e✔eryday
Comprehension
Intervention Activities

Table of Contents

Using Everyday Comprehension Intervention Activities

Reading with full text comprehension is the ultimate goal of all reading instruction. Students who read the words but don't comprehend them aren't really reading at all. Research has shown that explicit comprehension strategy instruction helps students understand and remember what they read, which allows them to communicate what they've learned with others and perform better in testing situations.

Although some students master comprehension strategies easily during regular classroom instruction, many others need additional re-teaching opportunities to master these essential strategies. The Everyday Intervention Activities series provides easy-to-use, five-day intervention units for Grades K–5. These units are structured around a research-based Model-Guide-Practice-Apply approach. You can use these activities in a variety of intervention models, including Response to Intervention (RTI).

Getting Started

In just five simple steps, Everyday Comprehension Intervention Activities provides everything you need to identify students' comprehension needs and to provide targeted, research-based intervention.

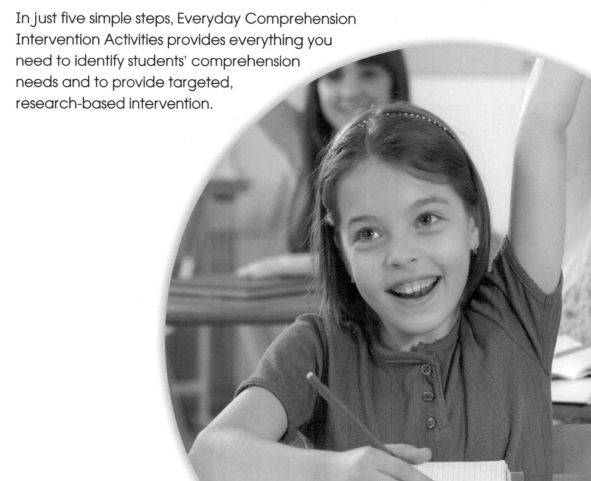

1. PRE-ASSESS to identify students' comprehension needs.

Use the pre-assessment on the CD-ROM to identify the strategies your students need to master.

2. MODEL the strategy.

Every five-day unit targets a specific strategy. On Day 1, use the teacher prompts and reproducible activity to introduce and model the strategy.

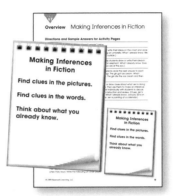

Day 1

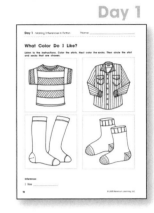

3. GUIDE PRACTICE and APPLY.

Use the reproducible practice activities for Days 2, 3, and 4 to build students' understanding of, and proficiency with, the strategy.

Day 2   **Day 3**   **Day 4**

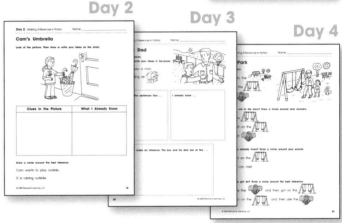

4. MONITOR progress.

Administer the Day 5 reproducible assessment to monitor each student's progress and to make instructional decisions.

Day 5

5. POST-ASSESS to document student progress.

Use the post-assessment on the CD-ROM to measure students' progress as a result of your interventions.

Standards-Based Comprehension Strategies in Everyday Intervention Activities

The comprehension strategies found in the Everyday Intervention Activities series are introduced developmentally and spiral from one grade to the next based on curriculum standards across a variety of states. The chart below shows the comprehension strategies addressed at each grade level in this series.

Comprehension Strategy	Strategy Definition	K	1	2	3	4	5
Make Predictions	Determine what might happen next in a story or nonfiction piece. Predictions are based on information presented in the text.	✔	✔	✔	✔	✔	✔
Identify Sequence of Events	Determine the order of events for topics such as history, science, or biography. Determine the steps to make or do something.	✔	✔	✔	✔	✔	✔
Analyze Story Elements	Analyze the setting and plot (problem/solution) in a fiction text.	✔	✔	✔	✔	✔	✔
Analyze Character	Analyze story characters based on information and on clues and evidence in the text, including description, actions, dialogue, feelings, and traits.	✔	✔	✔	✔	✔	✔
Identify Main Idea and Supporting Details	Determine what the paragraph, page, or chapter is mostly about. Sometimes the main idea is stated and sometimes it is implied. Students must choose details that support the main idea, not "just any detail."	✔	✔	✔	✔	✔	✔
Summarize	Take key ideas from the text and put them together to create a shorter version of the original text. Summaries should have few, if any, details.	✔	✔	✔	✔	✔	✔
Compare and Contrast	Find ways that two things are alike and different.	✔	✔	✔	✔	✔	✔
Identify Cause and Effect	Find things that happened (effect) and why they happened (cause). Text may contain multiple causes and effects.	✔	✔	✔	✔	✔	✔
Make Inferences	Determine what the author is suggesting without directly stating it. Inferences are usually made during reading and are made from one or two pieces of information from the text. Students' inferences will vary but must be made from the evidence in the text and background knowledge.	✔	✔	✔	✔	✔	✔
Draw Conclusions	Determine what the author is suggesting without directly stating it. Conclusions are made during and after reading, and are made from multiple (3+) pieces of information from the text. Students' conclusions will vary but must be drawn from the evidence in the text and background knowledge.		✔	✔	✔	✔	✔
Evaluate Author's Purpose	Determine why the author wrote the passage or used certain information. A book can have more than one purpose. Purposes include to entertain, to inform, and to persuade.			✔	✔	✔	✔
Analyze Text Structure and Organization	Determine the text structure to better understand what the author is saying and to use as research when text must be analyzed.			✔	✔	✔	✔
Use Text Features to Locate Information	Use text features (bullets, captions, glossary, index, sidebars) to enhance meaning.			✔	✔	✔	✔
Use Graphic Features to Interpret Information	Use clues from graphic features (charts, maps, graphs) to determine what is not stated in the text or to enhance meaning.			✔	✔	✔	✔
Distinguish and Evaluate Facts and Opinions	Recognize objective statements of fact and subjective opinions within a nonfiction text.					✔	✔
Make Judgments	Use facts from the text and prior knowledge and beliefs to make and confirm opinions about the characters or situations.					✔	✔

Everyday Comprehension Intervention Activities Grade 1 • ©2010 Newmark Learning, LLC

Using Everyday Intervention for RTI

According to the National Center on Response to Intervention, RTI "integrates assessment and intervention within a multi-level prevention system to maximize student achievement and to reduce behavior problems." This model of instruction and assessment allows schools to identify at-risk students, monitor their progress, provide research-proven interventions, and "adjust the intensity and nature of those interventions depending on a student's responsiveness."

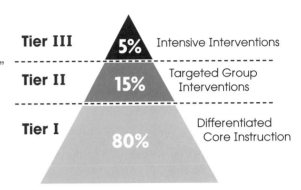

RTI models vary from district to district, but the most prevalent model is a three-tiered approach to instruction and assessment.

The Three Tiers of RTI	Using Everyday Intervention Activities
Tier I: Differentiated Core Instruction • Designed for all students • Preventive, proactive, standards-aligned instruction • Whole- and small-group differentiated instruction • Ninety-minute, daily core reading instruction in the five essential skill areas: phonics, phonemic awareness, comprehension, vocabulary, fluency	• Use whole-group comprehension mini-lessons to introduce and guide practice with comprehension strategies that all students need to learn. • Use any or all of the units in the order that supports your core instructional program.
Tier II: Targeted Group Interventions • For at-risk students • Provide thirty minutes of daily instruction beyond the ninety-minute Tier I core reading instruction • Instruction is conducted in small groups of three to five students with similar needs	• Select units based on your students' areas of need (the pre-assessment can help you identify these). • Use the units as week-long, small-group mini-lessons.
Tier III: Intensive Interventions • For high-risk students experiencing considerable difficulty in reading • Provide up to sixty minutes of additional intensive intervention each day in addition to the ninety-minute Tier I core reading instruction • More intense and explicit instruction • Instruction conducted individually or with smaller groups of one to three students with similar needs	• Select units based on your students' areas of need. • Use the units as one component of an intensive comprehension intervention program.

Overview Making Predictions in Fiction

Directions and Sample Answers for Activity Pages

Day 1	See "Provide a Real-World Example" below.
Day 2	Discuss the book cover. Ask students to predict what might be in a book called *A Gift for Dad*. Then help students color the pictures they predict might be in the book. (watch, drill, tie, "I love you" card, dad)
Day 3	Read and discuss each page. Then help students draw or write what they predict will happen next. (**Star friend with jump rope:** Two stars will twirl the rope and one will jump over it. **Star friend with paper and markers:** The three star friends will draw together.)
Day 4	Read and discuss each clue. Then ask students to predict who Detective Bing might talk to about the clue and draw a line to that character. (**Clue about footprints:** barefoot girl. **Clue about hole in the yard:** kids with shovel. **Clue about cake crumbs:** boy with chocolate on his face.)
Day 5	Read the story together. Ask students to draw or write what they predict the fox will do. Afterward, meet individually with students to discuss their results. Use their responses to plan further instruction and review. (**Clues:** "Please stay. You will like it here." **Prediction:** The fox will live in the forest.)

Provide a Real-World Example

◆ Hand out the Day 1 activity page.

◆ **Say:** *My friend likes to take pictures with his camera. On Saturday, he is going to the zoo. You can predict—or make a good guess about—what types of pictures my friend will take at the zoo. Look at the top row of pictures. Which ones do you predict my friend might take?*

◆ Allow time for students to color the correct pictures. Then repeat the process on the second row with pictures they predict your friend might take when visiting someone's home and on the third row with pictures they predict your friend might take when visiting the library.

◆ Invite students to share their predictions with a partner, including why they made each prediction. Then explain that they can also make predictions when they read. Write the following on chart paper:

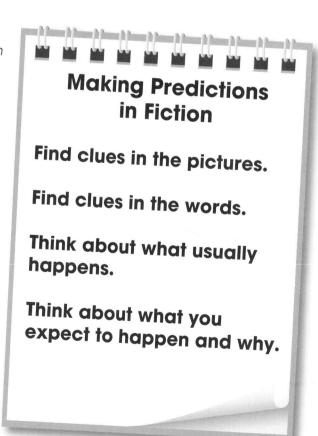

Making Predictions in Fiction

Find clues in the pictures.

Find clues in the words.

Think about what usually happens.

Think about what you expect to happen and why.

Taking Pictures

Which photos would someone take at the zoo?

Which photos would someone take at the house?

Which photos would someone take at the library?

A Gift for Dad

Look at the cover of this book.

Color the pictures you predict will be in this story.

Star Friends

Read each page. Predict what you think will happen next in the story.

Detective Bing's Case

Read the passage.

 has a case. found some clues.

Detective Bing   Detective Bing

Read each clue.

Then predict who will talk to about the clue.

Detective Bing

Draw a line to connect the person to the clue.

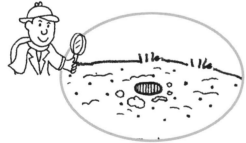

Assessment

Read the passage. Write down the clues. Then make a prediction.

A fox visited a forest.

"Please stay. You will like it here," said Ant.

"Please stay. You will like it here," said Owl.

"Please stay. You will like it here," said Bear.

"Yes, please stay!" said the other animals. "You will like it here!"

Clues	Prediction

Overview Making Predictions in Nonfiction

Directions and Sample Answers for Activity Pages

Day 1	See "Provide a Real-World Example" below.
Day 2	Discuss the book cover. Ask students to predict what might be in a book called *At the Pond*. Then help students color the pictures they predict might be in the book. (fish, rowboat, cattails, dragonfly)
Day 3	Read and discuss each page. Then help students draw or write what they predict will happen next. (**Girl filling dog's bowl:** A dog will eat the food. **Boy with bucket and sponge:** The boy will wash a car.)
Day 4	Read and discuss each e-mail. Ask students to predict who might get the e-mail. Then help students draw a line to match each message to its predicted recipient. (**E-mail about park:** kids. **E-mail about Jon:** teacher. **E-mail about gift:** grandparent.)
Day 5	Read the sign together. Ask students to draw or write what they predict will happen when people read the sign. Afterward, meet individually with students to discuss their results. Use their responses to plan further instruction and review. (**Evidence:** Summer, 10¢ a glass, free pretzel. **Prediction:** Many people will buy a glass of lemonade.)

Provide a Real-World Example

◆ Hand out the Day 1 activity page.

◆ **Say:** *We are at school. We are having reading class. What do we usually do right after reading class? What do you predict we will do after reading class today?*

◆ Allow time for students to draw or write their predictions beside the picture of a student in reading class.

◆ Repeat the process by having students predict what they will do right after lunch and right after school.

◆ Invite students to share their predictions with a partner, including why they made each prediction. Then explain that they can also make predictions when they read. Write the following on chart paper:

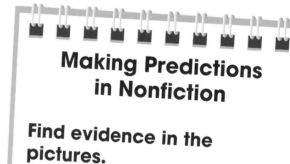

Making Predictions in Nonfiction

Find evidence in the pictures.

Find evidence in the words.

Think about what usually happens.

Think about what you expect to happen and why.

Right After

What do you predict will happen next? Draw your prediction in the box.

At the Pond

Look at the cover of this book. Then color
the pictures you predict will be in this book.

Doing Jobs at Home

Read the page. Then predict what you think will happen next in the book.

Kids can feed the dog.

Kids can wash the car.

E-mail

Read each e-mail. Predict who you think will get the e-mail.
Draw a line from the e-mail to the person.

Do you want to go to
the park? Call me!

Jon is sick. He will not
be at school today.

Thank you for the gift.
I had a fun birthday!

Assessment

Read the sign. First draw or write the evidence. Then draw or write your prediction.

Summer is here!
LEMONADE
10¢ a glass!
FREE Pretzel with each glass

Evidence	Prediction

Overview Identifying Sequence of Events in Fiction

Directions and Sample Answers for Activity Pages

Day 1	See "Provide a Real-World Example" below.
Day 2	Discuss each picture. Then help students cut out the pictures, put them in the correct order, and glue them onto another sheet of paper. (eating pancakes at breakfast, reading a story at school, playing soccer after school, camping out at night)
Day 3	Discuss the pictures in each row. Then help students determine what they could draw to complete each sequence of events. (**Top row:** birthday cake with lit candle. **Middle row:** someone opening the door for the boy in costume. **Bottom row:** candy falling out of the piñata.)
Day 4	Discuss the pictures. Then help students number the sentences in the correct order. (3, 2, 4, 1)
Day 5	Read the story together. Ask students to write or draw the events in order on the graphic organizer. Afterward, meet individually with students to discuss their results. Use their responses to plan further instruction and review. (Vic was sad, Kim called, Vic went to Kim's house, Vic was happy)

Provide a Real-World Example

◆ Hand out the Day 1 activity page.

◆ **Say:** *Once I was going to the beach. First, I got my sun hat. Next, I got my sunglasses. Then I got my towel. After that, I put everything in my beach bag. Finally, I drove to the beach. Doing things in a certain order is called a sequence of events.*

◆ Remind students that the first thing you got was your sun hat. Ask them to locate the sun hat on their page and write **1** in the box. Repeat the process with the sunglasses (**2**) and towel (**3**).

◆ **Say:** *Now look at the next row of pictures. Think about the story I just told. Put **1** on the picture that shows what is in my bag of things for the beach. Put **2** on the picture that shows what happened after I got these things. Put **3** on the picture that shows what happened last.*

◆ Discuss students' responses. Then explain that they can also find a sequence of events when they read. Write the following on chart paper:

Identifying Sequence of Events in Fiction

Find clues in the pictures.

Find words that tell about order, such as *first, then, next,* and *last*.

Think about the order in which things usually happen.

Going to the Beach

Number the pictures below in the correct order.

Kay's Fun Day

Cut out the pictures. Put them in the correct order.

Then glue them onto another sheet of paper.

Party Time

Draw a picture to show what comes first, next, or last.

Toby Gets a Book

Toby wanted a book about dogs. Look at the pictures.

First

Next

Then

Last

Number the sentences in the correct order.

[ ] Toby went home.

[ ] Toby got a book.

[ ] Toby read to Moe.

[ ] Toby went to the library.

Assessment

Read the story. Then write or draw the events of the story in the correct order.

Vic was [sad] . Vic could not find his [ball] .

Then the [phone] rang. "Can you come to my [house] ?" asked Kim.

"We can play with my [ball] ."

Vic went to Kim's [house] . Vic was [happy] at last!

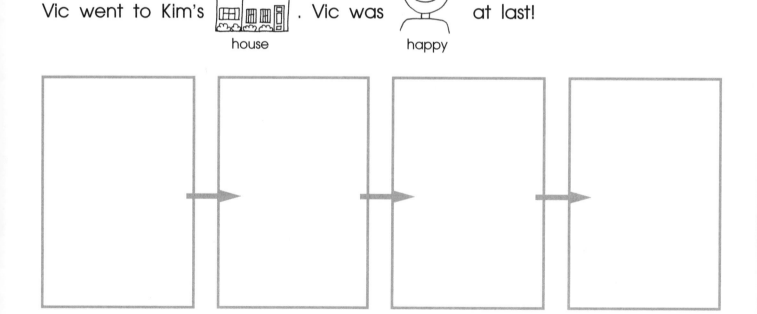

Overview Identifying Sequence of Events in Nonfiction

Directions and Sample Answers for Activity Pages

Day 1	See "Provide a Real-World Example" below.
Day 2	Discuss each picture. Then help students cut out the pictures, put them in the correct order, and glue them onto another sheet of paper. (planting seed, watering plant, plant starting to sprout, fully-grown plant with flower)
Day 3	Discuss the pictures in each row. Then help students determine what they need to draw to complete each sequence of events. (**Top row:** a clock that says 1:00. **Middle row:** someone using a key to unlock the door. **Bottom row:** someone cutting or eating the cake.)
Day 4	Discuss the pictures. Then help students number the sentences in the correct order. (3, 1, 4, 2)
Day 5	Read the passage together. Ask students to write or draw the events in order on the graphic organizer. Afterward, meet individually with students to discuss their results. Use their responses to plan further instruction and review. (put soap on hands, rub hands together, rinse hands, dry hands)

Provide a Real-World Example

◆ Hand out the Day 1 activity page.

◆ **Say:** *Once I had some coins in a jar. First, I counted the dimes. Next, I counted the nickels. Then I counted the pennies. After that, I put the coins in my pocket. Finally, I used the coins to buy bread. Doing things in a certain order is called a sequence of events.*

◆ Remind students that the first coins you counted were dimes. Ask them to locate the dime on their page and write **1** in the box. Repeat the process with the nickel (**2**) and penny (**3**).

◆ **Say:** *Now look at the next row of pictures. Think about the story I just told. Put 1 on the picture that shows the coins before I counted them. Put 2 on the picture that shows what happened after I counted the coins. Put 3 on the picture that shows what happened last.*

◆ Discuss students' responses. Then explain that they can also find a sequence of events when they read. Write the following on chart paper:

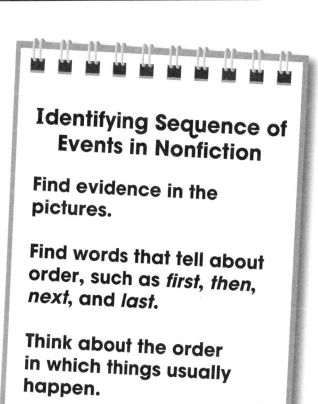

Identifying Sequence of Events in Nonfiction

Find evidence in the pictures.

Find words that tell about order, such as *first*, *then*, *next*, and *last*.

Think about the order in which things usually happen.

Counting Coins

Listen to the example. Then number the pictures in the correct order.

nickel

dime

penny

Listen. Then number in the correct order.

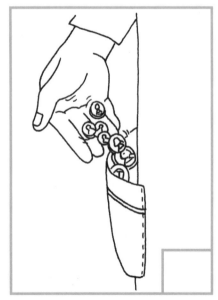

Growing a Flower

Cut out the pictures. Put them in the correct order.

Then glue them onto another sheet of paper.

First, Next, and Last

Draw a picture to show what comes first, next, or last.

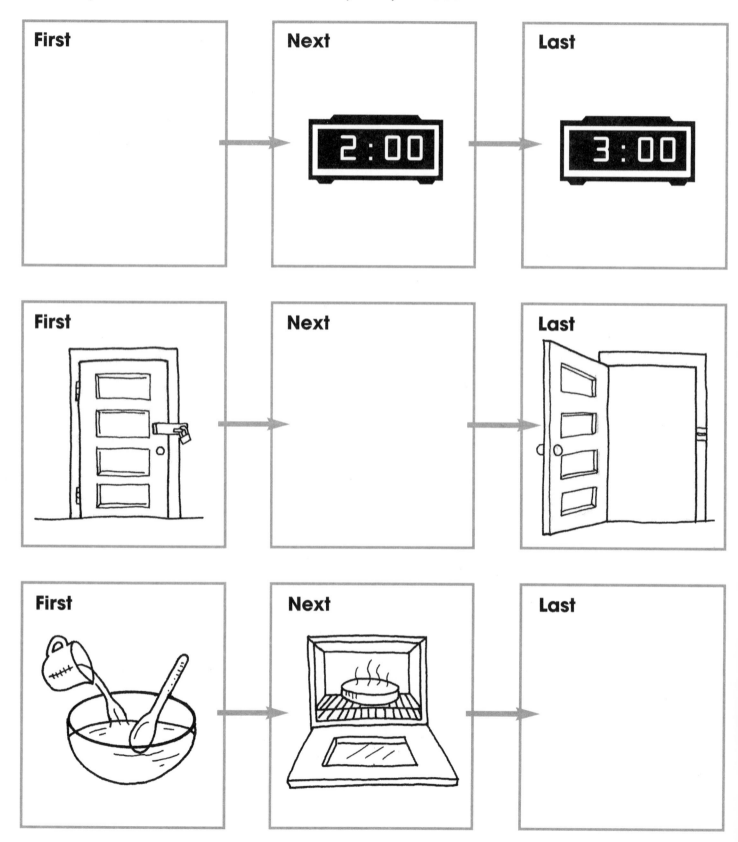

 Unit 4 • Everyday Comprehension Intervention Activities Grade 1 • ©2010 Newmark Learning, LLC

Going Places

People made new ways to go places. Look at the pictures.

First

Next

Then

Last

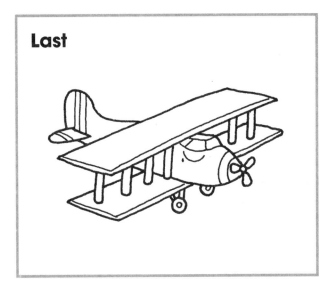

Number the sentences in the correct order.

☐ People made cars.

☐ People made wagons.

☐ People made planes.

☐ People made trains.

Assessment

Read the passage.

How do you wash your  ?
hands

First, put  on your wet  .
soap   hands

Then rub your together while you count to 15.
hands

Next, rinse your with clean  .
hands   water

Last, dry your hands with a clean  .
towel

Draw each step in the process.

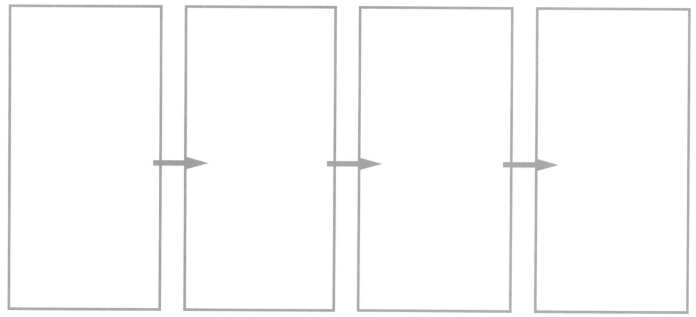

Overview Analyzing Story Elements: Setting

Directions and Sample Answers for Activity Pages

Day 1	See "Provide a Real-World Example" below.
Day 2	Discuss each picture. Then help students name the setting, find the word in the Word Bank, and write it on the line. (**Bridge over water:** lake. **Jungle gym:** park. **Girl with cat:** yard. **Rocket:** space.)
Day 3	Read the book titles together. Discuss what types of settings could be in each book. Help students draw a line from each book to an appropriate setting. (*New Girl at School*: cafeteria. *Cal's Clubhouse*: tree house. *The Long Winter*: tree branch. *A Birthday Cake for Mom*: kitchen.)
Day 4	Discuss things that could have happened long ago, last year, last night, and this morning. Discuss where these things could have happened. Remind students that the settings can be real or imaginary. Then help students draw their ideas in the boxes and write the place names underneath. (Responses will vary.)
Day 5	Read the passage together. Ask students to record the setting clues and setting on their graphic organizers. Afterward, meet individually with students to discuss their results. Use their responses to plan further instruction and review. (**Clues:** kitchen, chair, bed. **Setting:** day and night in a house where people live.)

Provide a Real-World Example

◆ Hand out the Day 1 activity page.

◆ **Say:** *Today we will talk about setting. A setting is when and where something takes place.*

◆ Ask students to pretend they are on a trip. Invite them to close their eyes and listen as you describe the setting. **Say:** *The sun is shining. You hear waves crashing on the ocean. You smell hot dogs cooking. You see children building a sand castle.*

◆ Ask students to open their eyes and color the pictures that are a part of the setting you described. Then help them determine that it is daytime and they are at the beach.

◆ Explain that they can also analyze settings when they read. Write the following on chart paper:

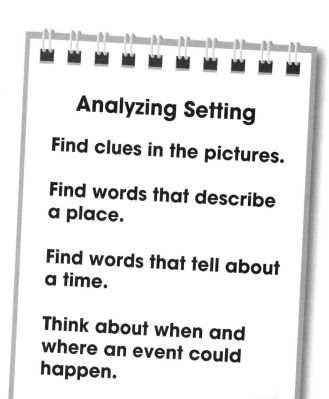

Analyzing Setting

Find clues in the pictures.

Find words that describe a place.

Find words that tell about a time.

Think about when and where an event could happen.

On a Trip

Listen to the description. Then color the pictures that are part of this setting.

Circle the correct choice.

It is _____.   summer   winter   fall   spring

You are at the _____.   playground   beach   lake

Places

Look at the pictures. Find the name of each place in the Word Bank.

Write the name of the place on the line.

Word Bank			
yard	park	space	lake

_____   _____

_____   _____

Setting Match

Read each book title. Draw a line to a setting that could be in the book.

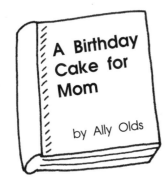

When and Where

Draw something that could have happened.

Write where it could have happened.

When: Long ago

Where: _____

When: Last year

Where: _____

When: Last night

Where: _____

When: This morning

Where: _____

Assessment

Read the passage. Then record the clues and setting in the boxes below.

Spot eats in a  .

kitchen

Spot sits on a .

chair

Spot sleeps on a .

bed

Spot loves his home!

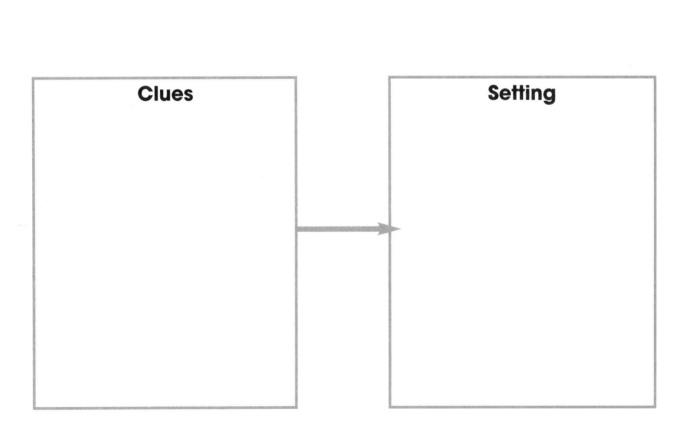

Clues	Setting

Overview Analyzing Story Elements: Plot

Directions and Sample Answers for Activity Pages

Day 1	See "Provide a Real-World Example" below.
Day 2	Together, read and discuss the beginning and end of each story. Then help students draw or write what could happen in the middle. (Responses will vary.)
Day 3	Discuss each picture. Ask students to color the picture if it shows a problem that could be in a story. (muddy dog, biting bug, angry boy, turtle going after hippo)
Day 4	Read the beginning and middle of the story together. Discuss. Then help students circle the best ending to the story. (Mya's sister put candles on the cake.)
Day 5	Read the story together. Ask students to write or draw what happened at the beginning, middle, and end of the story on their graphic organizers. Afterward, meet individually with students to discuss their results. Use their responses to plan further instruction and review. (**Beginning:** Roy had a white coat. He wanted a red coat. **Middle:** Roy asked Fox for his red coat. Fox said he would eat Roy for dinner. **End:** Roy ran home. He likes his white coat now.)

Provide a Real-World Example

◆ Hand out the Day 1 activity page.

◆ **Say:** *I lost my pencil. I will look for my pencil.* Look in several different places before "finding" your pencil.

◆ **Say:** *Losing and finding my pencil is like a story. At the beginning, I had a problem. I lost my pencil.*

◆ Ask students to find the box that tells the **b**eginning of the story and put a **B** beside it.

◆ **Say:** *In the middle of the story, I tried to solve my problem. I looked for my pencil.*

◆ Ask students to find the box that tells the **m**iddle of the story and put an **M** beside it.

◆ **Say:** *At the end of the story, I solved my problem. I found my pencil.*

◆ Ask students to find the box that tells the **e**nd of the story and put an **E** beside it.

◆ Tell students that the parts of a story are called the plot. Then explain that they can also analyze plots they read. Write the following on chart paper:

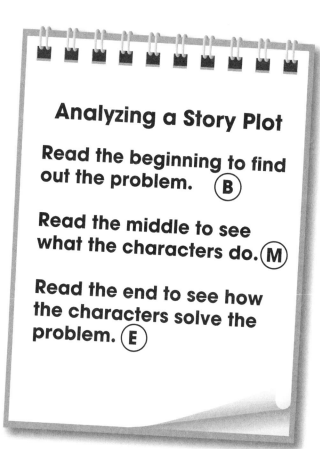

Analyzing a Story Plot

Read the beginning to find out the problem. (B)

Read the middle to see what the characters do. (M)

Read the end to see how the characters solve the problem. (E)

The Missing Pencil

Listen to the example. Then label each sentence   .

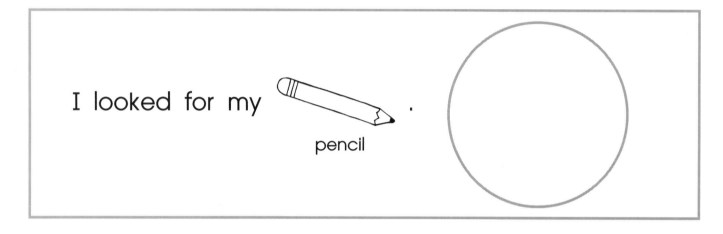

I looked for my [pencil] .

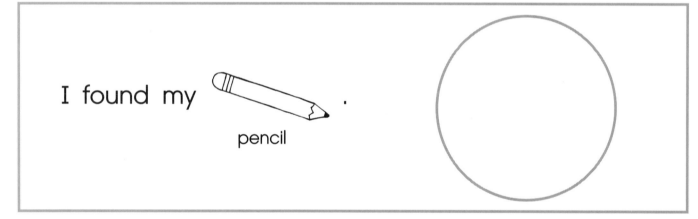

I found my [pencil] .

I lost my [pencil] .

In the Middle

Read the beginning and end of each story.

Then draw or write what could happen in the middle.

"I don't want to go to bed," said Ava.

Good night, Ava!

"I'm hungry," said Bear.

"Thank you, Squirrel!" said Bear.

Name _____

Problems!

Look at each picture.

Color the picture if it shows a problem that could be in a story.

Unit 6 • Everyday Comprehension Intervention Activities Grade 1 • ©2010 Newmark Learning, LLC

The Cake

Read the beginning and middle of the story.

Then draw a circle around the best ending.

Beginning

Mya's sister made a .

cake

"It does not look like a birthday ," said Mya.

cake

Middle

Mya's sister put icing on the .

cake

"That looks nice.

But it does not look like a birthday ," said Mya.

cake

End

Mya put more icing on the .

cake

"All better!" said Mya.

Mya's sister put  on the .

candles   cake

"All better!" said Mya.

Mya and her sister ate the .

birthday cake

"All better!" said Mya.

Assessment

"We are alike," said Roy.

"We have white coats," said Rex.

"I want a red coat," said Roy.

Roy went to Fox.

"May I have your red coat?" asked Roy.

"No!" said Fox. "But I will have you for dinner!"

Roy ran home. "I like our white coats," he said.

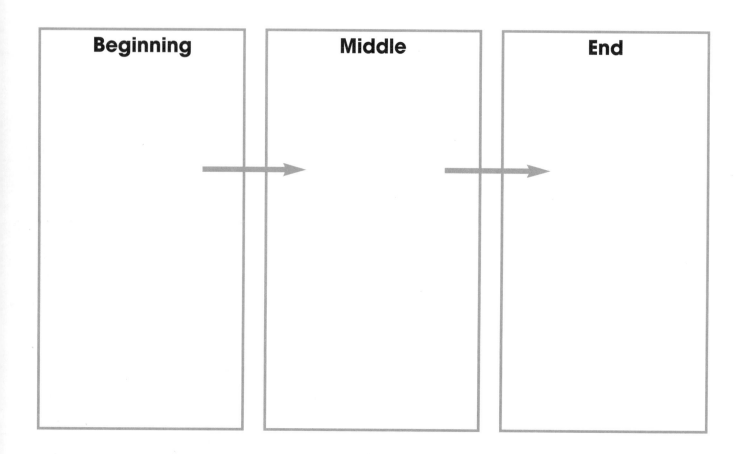

Beginning	Middle	End

Overview Analyzing Character: Traits

Directions and Sample Answers for Activity Pages

Day 1	See "Provide a Real-World Example" below.
Day 2	Ask each student to think of two people at school, such as students, teachers, secretaries, or custodians. Help them fill in the sentences to name a trait each person has. Then ask them to draw a picture that shows each person's trait in action. (Responses will vary.)
Day 3	Read the story together. Discuss the clues in the story that show Mae's traits. Then help students circle the correct answer to each question. (kind, helpful, reliable)
Day 4	Read the story together. Discuss the clues in the story that show the characters' traits. Then help students circle Dog's and Cat's traits at the beginning and end of the story. (**Dog:** friendly, then mean. **Cat:** polite, then angry.)
Day 5	Read the story together. Ask students to write or draw clues about one of the character's traits and name the trait on their graphic organizers. Afterward, meet individually with students to discuss their results. Use their responses to plan further instruction and review. (**Clues about king:** beautiful day, read a good book, have a big party. **Trait:** cheerful. **Clues about princess:** raining, bored, stay in my room. **Trait:** grumpy.)

Provide a Real-World Example

◆ Hand out the Day 1 activity page.

◆ **Say:** *I saw a friend a few days ago. My friend just started a new job. She said she was very shy at first. What does it mean to be shy?*

◆ Allow time for students to discuss what it means to be shy. Then **say:** *Being shy is a characteristic, or trait, of many people. Write or draw a picture of a time you have been shy.*

◆ Repeat the process with the traits of being friendly and being funny.

◆ Allow time for students to share their ideas. Then explain that they can also analyze character traits when they read. Write the following on chart paper:

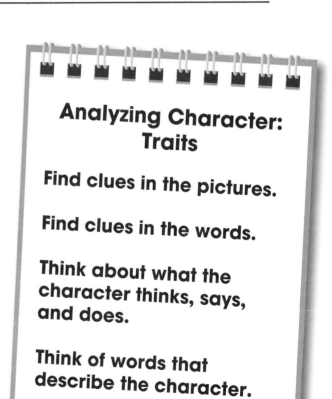

Analyzing Character: Traits

Find clues in the pictures.

Find clues in the words.

Think about what the character thinks, says, and does.

Think of words that describe the character.

Shy, Friendly, and Funny

Listen to the example. Then write or draw your own examples of being shy, friendly, and funny.

I was shy when . . .

I was friendly when . . .

I was funny when . . .

Name _____

People at School

Think of two people at school.
Tell who each person is. Then name
a trait each person has. Then draw a
picture of each person that shows the trait.

_____
(name of person)

is _____.
(trait)

_____
(name of person)

is _____.
(trait)

Yard Sale

Read the story.

"We will have a yard sale," said Mom. "That will be fun!" said Mae.

Mae set up 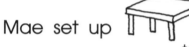 . Mae put out .
tables books

Mae put out  . Mae put out  .
toys clothes

Many  came. Mae helped the  .
people people

"We made lots of ," said Mom. "Thank you, Mae!"
money

Think about Mae's traits. Draw a circle around the best answers.

Is Mae kind?	Yes	No
Is Mae helpful?	Yes	No
Is Mae mean?	Yes	No
Is Mae lazy?	Yes	No
Is Mae reliable?	Yes	No
Is Mae greedy?	Yes	No

Why Cats and Dogs Aren't Friends

Read the story.

"Let's play tag," said Dog.

"Purr . . . fect," said Cat.

"Now, let's play ball," said Dog.

"Purr . . . fect," said Cat.

"Now, let's play a game," said Dog.

"Purr . . . OW!" said Cat.

"Stop biting me!"

"Ha, ha!" said Dog.

Now, cats and dogs are no longer friends.

Think about the animals' traits at the beginning and end of the story. Draw a circle around the best answers.

At first, Dog was _____.	friendly	messy
Then Dog was _____.	calm	mean
At first, Cat was _____.	bossy	polite
Then Cat was _____.	angry	patient

Assessment

Read the story.

"Oh, what a beautiful day," said the  .
King

"It's raining," said the .
Queen

"I'm going to read a good book," said the  .
King

"I'm going to be bored," said the 🜲 .
Queen

"Then I'm going to have a big party," said the 🜲 .
King

"I'm going to stay in my room," said the 🜲 .
Queen

Choose a character. Then draw or write the clues and the traits of that character.

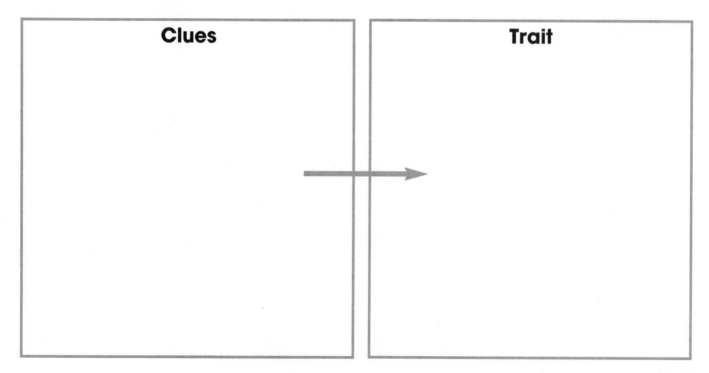

Clues	Trait

Overview Analyzing Character: Feelings

Directions and Sample Answers for Activity Pages

Day 1	See "Provide a Real-World Example" below.
Day 2	Ask students to draw pictures of themselves doing something they like to do and something they don't like to do. Then help them fill in the sentences to name their feelings about each activity. (Responses will vary.)
Day 3	Read the story together. Discuss the clues in the story that show how Sam feels. Then help students draw a line from the sentence to the picture that shows how Sam felt at different points in the story. (**First:** surprised. **Then:** angry. **Finally:** happy.)
Day 4	Read the story together. Discuss the clues in the story that show how the characters feel. Then help students circle the correct answer to each question. (**Tad:** sad. **Mom:** worried. **Dee:** calm. **Rags:** frightened. **All, at the end:** happy.)
Day 5	Read each group of sentences together. Ask students to write or draw clues about one of the character's feelings and name the feeling on their graphic organizers. Afterward, meet individually with students to discuss their results. Use their responses to plan further instruction and review. (**Clues about Missy:** smart, teacher loved story. **Feeling:** proud. **Clues about Marty:** need a nap, lie on the sofa. **Feeling:** tired. **Clues about May:** miss friends, wish we didn't have to move. **Feeling:** lonely.)

Provide a Real-World Example

◆ Hand out the Day 1 activity page.

◆ **Say:** *Once I saw a little girl run out into the street. I felt so scared until I saw the girl's dad rescue her! What does it mean to feel scared?*

◆ Allow time for students to discuss what it means to feel scared. Then **say:** *Everyone feels scared sometimes. Write or draw a picture of a time you felt scared.*

◆ Repeat the process with feeling excited and feeling surprised.

◆ Allow time for students to share their ideas. Then explain that they can also analyze characters' feelings when they read. Write the following on chart paper:

Analyzing Character: Feelings

Find clues in the pictures.

Find clues in the words.

Think about what the character thinks, says, and does.

Think of words that describe how the character feels.

Scared, Excited, and Surprised

Listen to the example. Then draw or write your own examples of feeling scared, excited, and surprised.

I felt scared when . . .

I felt excited when . . .

I felt surprised when . . .

My Feelings

Draw a picture of yourself doing something you like to do. Then draw a picture of yourself doing something you don't like to do. Fill in the sentences to name your feelings.

Like	**Do Not Like**

I like to _____.

I feel _____

when I _____.

I don't like to _____.

I feel _____

when I _____.

Name _____

Sam the Squirrel

Read the story.

Knock! Knock! Sam opened his .
door

"Sid! I haven't seen you in years!" Sam said.

"I've come to live with you," said Sid.

"No! This is my !" said Sam.
tree

"But my is full of !" Sid said.
suitcase   acorns

"Welcome!" said Sam.

**Draw a line from the sentence to the picture that shows
how Sam felt.**

"Sid! I haven't seen you in years!"

"No! This is my !"
tree

"Welcome!"

The Lost Dog

Read the story.

Tad was crying. "I can't find Rags!"

"Oh no! Where can he be?" asked Mom.

"We'll find him!" said Dee.

Tad, Mom, and Dee looked for Rags.

Tad found Rags behind the bushes . Rags was shaking!

Tad, Mom, and Dee smiled and petted Rags.

Soon, Rags was wagging his tail .

How did the characters feel when Rags was lost?
Draw a circle around the best answers.

Tad felt _____.	sad	happy
Mom felt _____.	tired	worried
Dee felt _____.	lonely	calm
Rags felt _____.	frightened	proud

How did the characters feel when they found Rags?

angry   happy   upset

Assessment

Read the sentences. Choose a character.
Then draw or write about the character's feelings.

"I am smart!" said Missy.

"My  loved the story I wrote!"

teacher

Clues	**Feeling**

"I need a nap!" said Marty.

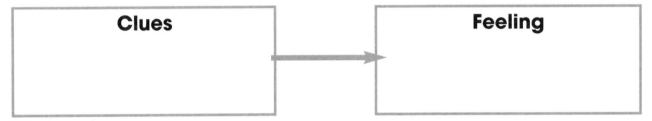
"I'm going to lie on the   and watch   ."
couch   television

Clues	**Feeling**

"I miss my friends," said May.

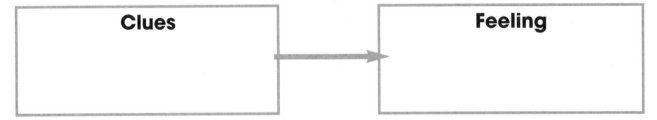
"I wish we didn't have to move to this new   ."
house

Clues	**Feeling**

Overview Identifying Stated Main Idea

Directions and Sample Answers for Activity Pages

Day 1	See "Provide a Real-World Example" below.
Day 2	Discuss each picture. Read the suggested main ideas. Then help students select and draw a circle around the best main idea for each picture. (**First:** The U.S. flag has stars and stripes. **Second:** People can get many things at a library.)
Day 3	Read the passage. Discuss. Help students select and color the stated main idea. Then ask them to draw a picture that goes with the stated main idea. (**Stated Main Idea:** A bike helmet helps keep you safe.)
Day 4	Read the passages together. Discuss. Then help students select and circle the stated main idea in each passage. (**First:** Many people have pets. **Second:** A gerbil needs good care.)
Day 5	Read the passage together. Ask students to read the supporting details in the second box on the graphic organizer. Then ask them to look back at the passage, find the stated main idea, and write it in the first box. Afterward, meet individually with students to discuss their results. Use their responses to plan further instruction and review. (**Stated Main Idea:** A compass rose shows directions on a map.)

Provide a Real-World Example

◆ Hand out the Day 1 activity page.

◆ **Say:** *My friend has a rock collection. One of the rocks is big. Write **big** under the first rock.*

◆ Allow time for students to write the word.

◆ **Say:** *One of the rocks is red. Color the middle rock red. Then write **red** on the line.*

◆ Allow time for students to color the middle rock and write the word.

◆ **Say:** *One of the rocks is bumpy. Write the word **bumpy** under the last rock.*

◆ Allow time for students to write the word under the last rock.

◆ **Say:** *A big rock, a red rock, and a bumpy rock are details in my friend's collection. What is the main idea I stated about this collection? Yes—my friend has a rock collection. Fill in the word **rock** to state the main idea.*

◆ Allow time for students to fill in the word. Then explain that they can also find stated main ideas when they read. Write the following on chart paper:

Identifying Stated Main Idea

See what the passage is about.

Find details about the topic.

Find the sentence that tells about the details.

Find the sentence that tells the most important idea.

The Collection

Listen to the example. Use the words below to describe each rock.
Then complete the sentence that states the main idea.

Word Bank

bumpy   rock   red   big

Details:

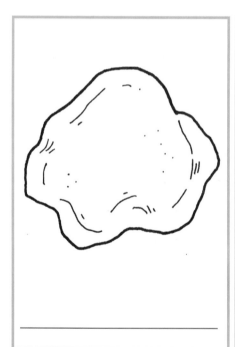

Main Idea:

My friend has a _____ collection.

Picture Main Ideas

Look at each picture. Draw a circle around the best main idea.

The U.S. flag has stars.

The U.S. flag has stripes.

The U.S. flag has stars and stripes.

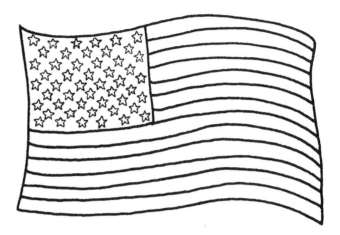

People can get many things at a library.

People can get books at a library.

People can get movies at a library.

Bike Helmets

Read the passage. Color the stated main idea.
Then draw a picture that goes with the stated main idea.

Do you wear a ?
helmet

A has a a hard top.
helmet

A helmet has a strap.

A helmet has a buckle.

A helmet should fit just right.

A helmet helps keep you safe.

Pets

Read each passage. Draw a circle around the stated main idea.

Many people have pets.

Some people have cats.

Some people have dogs.

Some people even have snakes!

What pet do you like best?

A gerbil needs food.

A gerbil needs water.

A gerbil needs a clean cage.

A gerbil needs good care.

Would you like to have a gerbil?

Assessment

Read the information below.

Have you ever seen a compass rose?

A compass rose shows directions on a map.

N shows north.

E shows east.

S shows south.

W shows west.

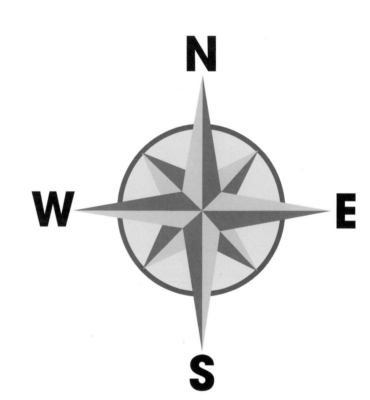

Write the stated main idea below.

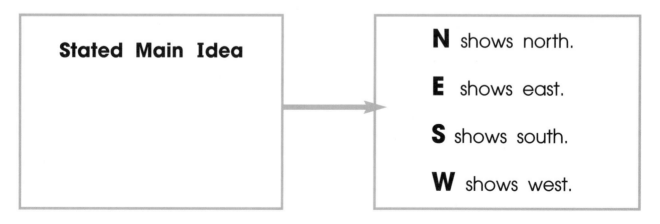

Overview Identifying Supporting Details

Directions and Sample Answers for Activity Pages

Day 1	See "Provide a Real-World Example" below.
Day 2	Discuss each picture. Read the suggested details. Then help students select and draw a circle around the details they see in the picture. (**First:** People take toy pails. People take toy shovels. **Second:** Get a toothbrush. Get some toothpaste.)
Day 3	Read the passage. Discuss. Help students select and color the supporting details. Then ask them to draw a picture that goes with the supporting details. (**Supporting details:** You can have a clock on the wall. You can have a clock on the dresser. You can have a watch on your wrist.)
Day 4	Read the passages together. Discuss. Then help students select and circle the supporting details in each passage. (**First:** Some kids have finger puppets. Some kids have sock puppets. Some kids have sack puppets. **Second:** You can move some puppets with your hand. You can move some puppets with sticks. You can move some puppets with strings.)
Day 5	Read the passage together. Ask students to write the stated main idea in the first box on the graphic organizer. Then ask them to write the supporting details in the second box. Afterward, meet individually with students to discuss their results. Use their responses to plan further instruction and review. (**Stated main idea:** People have jobs. **Supporting details:** Some people sell things. Some people make things. Some people take us places. Some people help us stay safe.)

Provide a Real-World Example

◆ Hand out the Day 1 activity page.

◆ Display a class list on a whiteboard or projector screen. **Say:** *I will state a main idea about this list: We are a class. Find the main idea on your page. Draw a circle around the stated main idea.*

◆ Allow time for students to locate and circle the stated main idea.

◆ **Say:** *Now we will write some details that support the main idea. Look at the names of the people in our class. Write a name on each line.*

◆ Allow time for students to write a classmate's name on each line.

◆ Invite students to read their supporting details to a partner. Then explain that they can also find supporting details when they read. Write the following on chart paper:

Identifying Supporting Details

See what the passage is about.

Find the sentence that tells the most important idea.

Find sentences that tell more information about the main idea.

Our Class

Draw a circle around the main idea.

We are a class.

_____ is in our class.

_____ is in our class.

_____ is in our class.

Picture Details

Look at each picture. Draw a circle around the details you see in the picture.

People take many things to the .
beach

People take 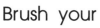.
towels

People take toy pails.

People take toy shovels.

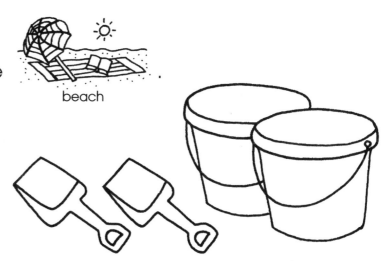

Get a toothbrush.

Get some .
water

Get some toothpaste.

Brush your .
teeth

Then go to .
bed

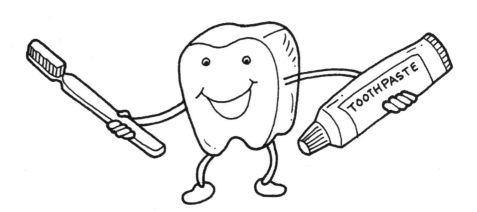

Telling Time

Read the passage. Color the supporting details.
Then draw a picture that goes with the supporting details.

People tell time in many ways.

You can have a clock on the 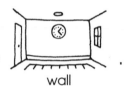 .

wall

You can have a clock on the  .

dresser

You can have a watch on your  .

wrist

Puppets

Read each passage. Draw a circle around the supporting details.

Do you like to play with puppets?

Kids have different kinds of puppets.

Some kids have finger puppets.

Some kids have sock puppets.

Some kids have sack puppets.

You can move some puppets with your hand.

You can move some puppets with sticks.

You can move some puppets with strings.

You can move puppets in many ways.

Assessment

Read the passage.

People have jobs.

Some people sell things.

Some people make things.

Some people take us places.

Some people help us stay safe.

What kind of job would you like best?

Write or draw the stated main idea and supporting details.

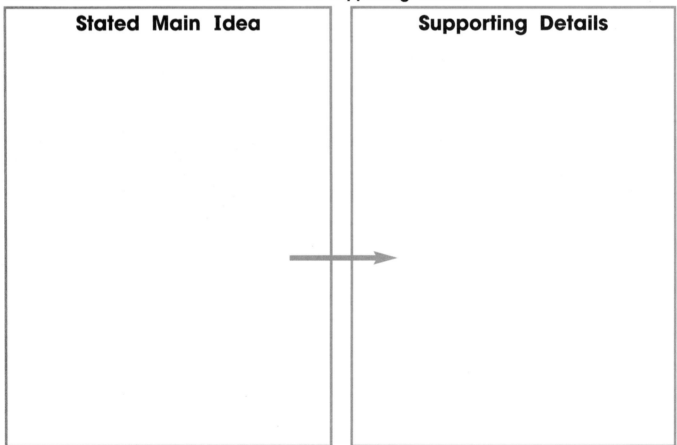

Stated Main Idea	Supporting Details

Overview Summarizing Fiction

Directions and Sample Answers for Activity Pages

Day 1	See "Provide a Real-World Example" below.
Day 2	Read each story. Discuss the big ideas. Then help students select and draw a circle around the best summary. (**First:** Liz shared the cookies. **Second:** Liz cleaned her room and read a book.)
Day 3	Read the story together. Discuss. Help students select and draw a line under the big ideas. Then help them fill in the missing words in the summary. (**Big Ideas:** Butterfly was having a party. Bird fell asleep. He missed the party! "I missed it, too," said Butterfly. "I fell asleep." **Summary:** Bird and Butterfly missed the party because they fell asleep.)
Day 4	Read the story together. Discuss. Help students write the big ideas in the squares and a summary in the circle. (**Big Ideas:** chef, firefighter, football player. **Summary:** Kip can be more than one thing.)
Day 5	Read the story together. Ask students to write or draw the big ideas and summary on their graphic organizers. Afterward, meet individually with students to discuss their results. Use their responses to plan further instruction and review. (**Big Ideas:** Whale bragged. Lobster bragged. Octopus bragged. Starfish bragged. Dolphin bragged. **Summary:** The sea animals bragged about who was best.)

Provide a Real-World Example

◆ Hand out the Day 1 activity page.

◆ **Say:** *My friend did many things yesterday. He went to work. He went to the store. He played tennis. He cleaned the house. Draw a circle around all the things my friend did.*

◆ Allow time for students to circle the correct activities. Repeat the description of your friend's day if needed.

◆ **Say:** *I can tell about my friend's day in one sentence: My friend had a busy day. This sentence is a summary. Fill in the last word to write a summary of my friend's day.*

◆ Allow time for students to write the word **day**. Invite them to read the summary to a partner. Then explain that they can also summarize stories they read. Write the following on chart paper:

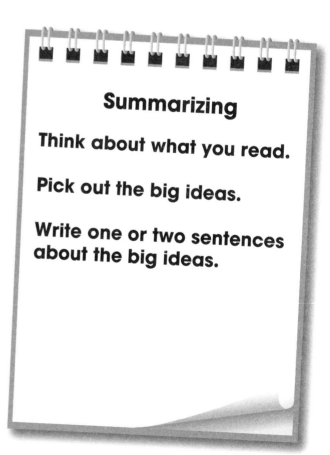

Summarizing

Think about what you read.

Pick out the big ideas.

Write one or two sentences about the big ideas.

My Friend's Day

Look at the pictures. Then complete the summary.

Summary:

My friend had a busy _____.

Liz

Read each story about Liz. Draw a circle around the best summary.

Liz had two  .

She saw Zoe. She saw Ted. She saw Wes.

Liz broke the  in half.

Everyone had a bite!

Summary:

Liz ate the _____ cookies .

Liz shared the _____ cookies .

Liz broke the _____ cookies .

Liz had a messy .
room

Liz picked up the 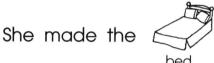 .
toys

She made the . She took out the .
bed   trash

"Now I can read a _____ !" said Liz.
book

Summary:

Liz made the _____ bed and took out the _____ trash .

Liz read a _____ book and picked up the _____ toys .

Liz cleaned her _____ room and read a _____ book .

The Party

Read the story. Draw a line under the big ideas.
Then fill in the missing words in the summary.

Bird got a 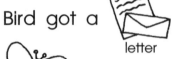 .

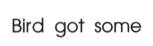 was having a party.

Bird got some to take.

Then Bird fell asleep.

He missed the party!

Bird took the to .

"I'm sorry I missed the party," said Bird.

"I missed it, too," said .

"I also fell asleep!"

Summary:

_____ and missed the _____

because they _____ .

What Will I Be?

Read the story.

"I don't know what I want to be," said Kip.

"Sometimes I want to be a  .
chef

Sometimes I want to be a  .
firefighter

Sometimes I want to be a  ."
football player

"You don't have to choose one," said Dad.

"You can be all three!"

Write the big ideas in the squares. Write a summary in the circle.

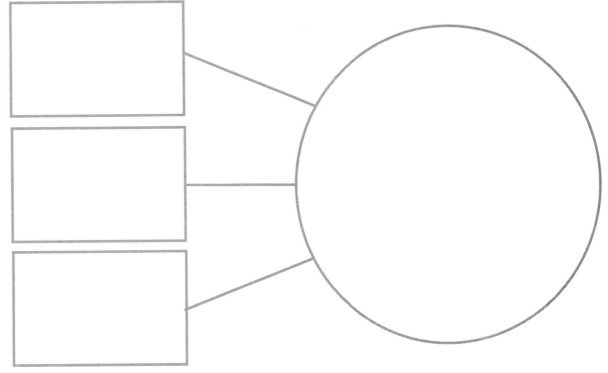

Assessment

Read the story.

One day, the sea animals were bragging.

"I'm big. I'm the best," said 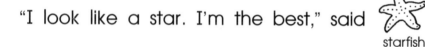 whale .

"I'm red. I'm the best," said lobster .

"I have 8 arms. I'm the best," said 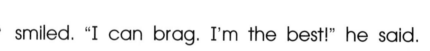 octopus .

"I look like a star. I'm the best," said starfish .

Dolphin smiled. "I can brag. I'm the best!" he said.

Draw or write the big ideas in this box.   **Draw or write a summary in this box.**

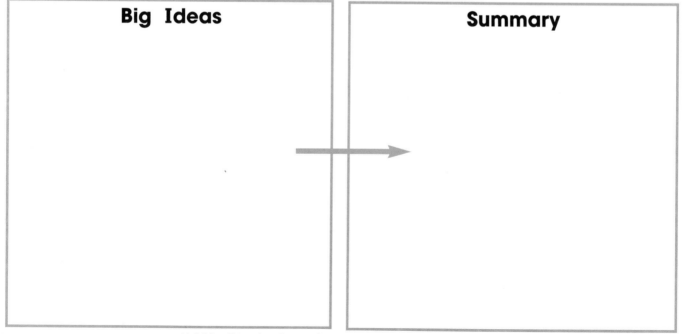

Big Ideas   **Summary**

Overview Summarizing Nonfiction

Directions and Sample Answers for Activity Pages

Day 1	See "Provide a Real-World Example" below.
Day 2	Read each passage. Discuss the big ideas. Then help students select and draw a circle around the best summary. (**First:** Animals have different homes. **Second:** Animals must live where they can get what they need.)
Day 3	Read the passage together. Discuss. Help students select and draw a line under the big ideas. Then help them fill in the missing words in the summary. (**Big Ideas:** The line on this thermometer is low. It is a cold day. The line on this thermometer is high. It is a hot day. **Summary:** A thermometer shows whether the day is cold or hot.)
Day 4	Read the ad together. Discuss. Help students write the big ideas in the squares and a summary in the circle. (**Big Ideas:** boy's bike, like new, $25. **Summary:** A boy wants to sell a nice bike for a good price.)
Day 5	Read the book review together. Ask students to write or draw the big ideas and summary on their graphic organizers. Afterward, meet individually with students to discuss their results. Use their responses to plan further instruction and review. (**Big Ideas:** *A Day at the Zoo*, map, photos, fun to read, learn a lot. **Summary:** *A Day at the Zoo* is an interesting book.)

Provide a Real-World Example

◆ Hand out the Day 1 activity page.

◆ **Say:** *Once I had three books in my backpack to read to the class. Then I put two more books in my backpack to return to the library. Count the books. How many did I have in all?*

◆ Allow time for students to count the books and write the number on the line.

◆ **Say:** *I can tell about the books in one sentence: I had five books in my backpack. This sentence is a summary. Fill in the line to write a summary about my books.*

◆ Allow time for students to write the numeral **5**. Invite them to read the summary to a partner. Then explain that they can also summarize when they read. Write the following on chart paper:

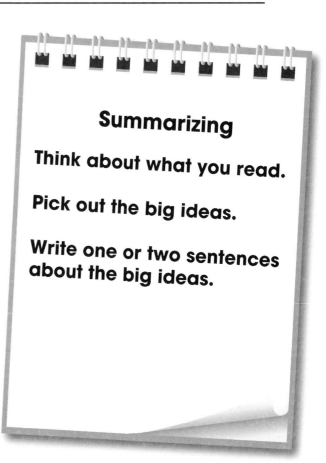

Summarizing

Think about what you read.

Pick out the big ideas.

Write one or two sentences about the big ideas.

Name _____

My Backpack

Count the books.

_____ books

Summary:

I had _____ books in my backpack.

Homes for Animals

Read each passage. Draw a circle around the best summary.

Animals have homes.

Some animals live in  .

Some animals live in .

Some animals live in the .

Animals live other places, too.

Summary: Animals have different homes.

Animals have homes in  and  .

The  is a home for animals.

An animal needs a good home.

The home must have food.

The home must have water.

The home must keep the animal safe.

Summary: Animals are safe in their homes.

Animals get food and water at home.

Animals must live where they can get what they need.

Thermometers

Read the passage. Draw a line under the big ideas. Then fill in the missing words in the summary.

The line on this is low.

thermometer

It is a cold day.

People wear .
coats

People make .
snowmen

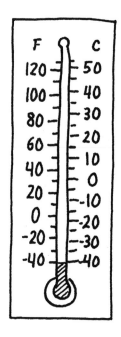

The line on this is high.
thermometer

It is a hot day.

People wear  .
light clothes

People go to the .
pool

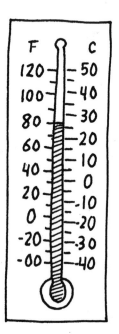

Summary: A shows if the day is _____ or _____ .
thermometer

Bike for Sale

Read the ad.

I have a boy's bike for sale.

The bike is like new.

It is too small for me now.

I got a bigger one for my birthday.

The price is $25.

You can see the bike at 202 North Main.

Write the big ideas in the squares. Write a summary in the circle.

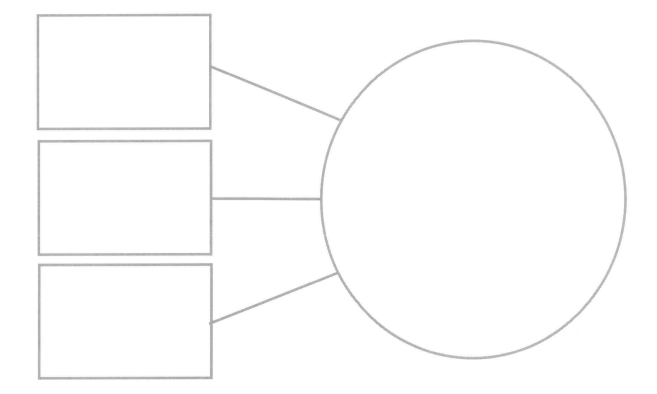

Assessment

Read the paper.

My Book Review

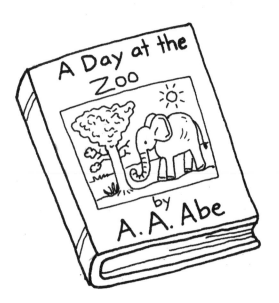

I read *A Day at the Zoo* by A. A. Abe.

The book has a map of the zoo.

The book has photos of zoo  .

animals

The book has photos of 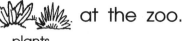 at the zoo.

plants

The book is fun to read.

Read it—you will learn a lot!

Draw or write the big ideas. Then draw or write a summary.

Big Ideas	**Summary**

Overview Comparing and Contrasting in Fiction

Directions and Sample Answers for Activity Pages

Day 1	See "Provide a Real-World Example" below.
Day 2	Discuss the picture. Then help students read the questions and circle the correct statements to show how the cat and dog are alike and different. (**Alike:** They both have a cake. **Different:** One has a crown. One has a cowboy hat.)
Day 3	Read the story together. Discuss the picture. Then help students mark the chart by placing an X in the appropriate column(s) to show how Pam and Pat are alike and different. (**Pam:** robot, her tool, likes to work, blocks, likes to play. **Pat:** robot, his tool, likes to work, soccer ball, likes to play.)
Day 4	Read the story together. Discuss the picture. Then help students circle the best answer to each question to show how Bud and Fay are alike and different. (**Bud:** I am in the sky. I am happy. **Fay:** I am in the lake. I am happy.)
Day 5	Read the story together. Ask students to write or draw what Meg likes to do, what Max likes to do, and what they both like to do. Afterward, meet individually with students to discuss their results. Use their responses to plan further instruction and review. (**Meg:** dig with hands. **Meg and Max:** play in the sandbox. **Max:** dig with a shovel.)

Provide a Real-World Example

◆ Hand out the Day 1 activity page.

◆ **Say:** *People live in many types of homes.* Point to the first home. **Say:** *Look at the first home. Does this home have a pointy roof? Yes!* Model how to draw a circle around the words **pointy roof** and the matching picture below the first home.

◆ Repeat the process with the door, windows, and flowers, making sure students do not circle **flowers**. Then repeat the process with the second home, making sure students do not circle **pointy roof**.

◆ **Say:** *We can compare these two homes. How are the homes alike?* Allow time for students to discuss that both homes have a door and windows.

◆ **Say:** *We can contrast these two homes. How are the homes different?* Allow time for students to discuss that only the first home has a pointy roof and only the second home has flowers.

◆ **Say:** *We can compare and contrast things when we read, too.* Write the following on chart paper:

Comparing and Contrasting in Fiction

Look at the pictures.

Think about the words.

See how things are alike. Look for words like *alike*, *both*, and *too*.

See how things are different. Look for words like *different*, *one*, and *but*.

Homes

Discuss how these homes are alike and different.

   pointy roof

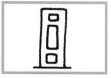   door

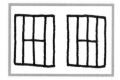   windows

   flowers

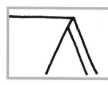   pointy roof

    door

   windows

   flowers

The Princess and the Cowboy

Look at the picture.

How are the cat and dog alike? Draw a circle around your answers.

They both have a .
crown

They both have a .
hat

They both have a .
cake

How are the cat and dog different? Draw a circle around your answers.

One has a .
crown

One has a .
hat

One has a .
cake

Pam and Pat

Read the story.

Pam and Pat are robots.

Pam and Pat like to work.

Pam and Pat like to play.

Mark the chart.

	Pam	Pat
robot		
has a 		
has a		
likes to work		
has		
has a		
likes to play		

   Unit 13 • Everyday Comprehension Intervention Activities Grade 1 • ©2010 Newmark Learning, LLC

Bud and Fay

Read the story.

Bud the  is in the  ,
bird   sky

but Fay the is in the  .
fish   lake

Bud the is .
bird   happy

Fay the is , too!
fish   happy

Draw a circle around your answers.

I am in the 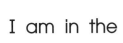 .
sky

bird   fish

I am in the 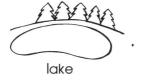 .
lake

bird   fish

I am .
happy

bird   fish

Assessment

Read the story

"I like to play in the  ," said Meg.

sandbox

"I do, too!" said Max.

"I like to dig with my ," said Meg.

hands

"I like to dig with a ," said Max.

shovel

Write or draw what Meg and Max like to do in the chart below.

Meg	Meg and Max	Max

Overview Comparing and Contrasting in Nonfiction

Directions and Sample Answers for Activity Pages

Day 1	See "Provide a Real-World Example" below.
Day 2	Read the sentences together. Discuss the pictures. Then help students read the questions and circle the correct statements to show how the two bikes are alike and different. (**Alike:** They both have a seat. They both have handlebars. **Different:** One has a bigger wheel in front. One has two wheels the same size.)
Day 3	Read the passage together. Discuss the pictures. Then help students mark the chart by placing an X in the appropriate column(s) to show how the street cone and jet are alike and different. (**Street cone:** a cone, on a street, helps people find their way. **Jet cone:** a cone, on a jet, helps a jet fly.)
Day 4	Read the passage together. Discuss the pictures. Then help students circle the best answer to each question to show how the boats are alike and different. (**Goes in water:** rowboat, ferryboat, cruise ship. **One person:** rowboat. **Many people:** ferryboat, cruise ship.)
Day 5	Read the passage together. Ask students to write or draw what they learned about a tree, what they learned about a raccoon, and what they learned about both. Afterward, meet individually with students to discuss their results. Use their responses to plan further instruction and review. (**Tree:** a plant. **Tree and raccoon:** lives in a forest; is alive. **Raccoon:** an animal.)

Provide a Real-World Example

◆ Hand out the Day 1 activity page.

◆ **Say:** *Many people like to eat pizza.* Point to the first pizza. **Say:** *Look at the first pizza. Does this pizza have pepperoni? Yes!* Model how to draw a circle around the word **pepperoni**.

◆ Repeat the process with the mushrooms and olives, making sure students do not circle **olives**. Then repeat the process with the second pizza, making sure students do not circle **mushrooms**. Finally, invite students to complete the sentences to describe each pizza's shape and size (round; big or small).

◆ **Say:** *We can compare these two pizzas. How are the pizzas alike?* Allow time for students to discuss that both pizzas have pepperoni and both are round.

◆ **Say:** *We can contrast these two pizzas. How are the pizzas different?* Allow time for students to discuss that the first pizza is big and has mushrooms, but the second pizza is small and has olives.

◆ **Say:** *We can compare and contrast things when we read, too.* Write the following on chart paper:

Comparing and Contrasting in Nonfiction

Look at the pictures.

Think about the words.

See how things are alike.
Look for words like *alike*, *both*, and *too*.

See how things are different.
Look for words like *different*, *one*, and *but*.

Pizza!

Discuss how the pizzas are alike and different.

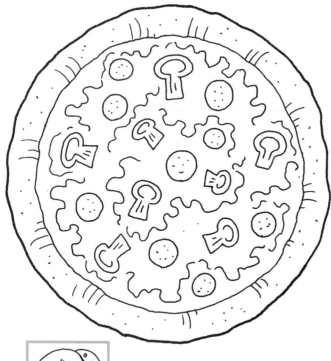 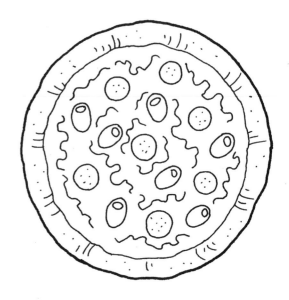

 pepperoni   pepperoni

 mushrooms   mushrooms

 olives   olives

Both pizzas are _____.

One pizza is _____ and

the other pizza is _____.

One pizza has _____ and

the other pizza has _____.

Bicycles

Read the sentences.

Look at the old bike.

Look at the new bike.

How are these bikes alike? Draw a circle around your answers.

They both have a seat.

They both have handlebars.

They both have a bigger wheel in front.

They both have two wheels the same size.

How are these bikes different? Draw a circle around your answers.

One has a seat.

One has handlebars.

One has a bigger wheel in front.

One has two wheels the same size.

Cones

Read the passage.

You can see cones all around.

You can see a cone on a jet.
The cone helps the jet fly.

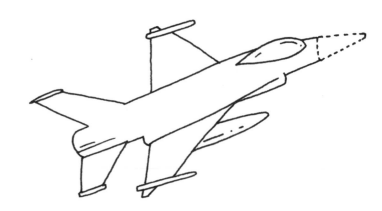

You can see cones on a street, too.
These cones help people find their way.

Mark the chart.

a cone		
on a street		
on a jet		
helps people find their way		
helps a jet fly		

Boats

Read the passage.

All boats go on water, but boats can be different sizes.

A rowboat is a small boat. One person can ride in this boat.

A  ferryboat is a big boat. Many people can ride in this boat.

A  cruise ship is even bigger. Many people can ride in this boat, too.

Draw a circle around your answers.

This boat goes in the water.

One person can ride in this boat.

Many people can ride in this boat.

Assessment

Read the passage.

A 🌲 lives in a forest. A 🦝 lives in a forest, too.
tree   raccoon

A 🌲 is alive. A 🦝 is alive, too.
tree   raccoon

A 🌲 is a plant, but a 🦝 is an animal.
tree   raccoon

How are the tree and the raccoon alike? How are they different? Write your answers in the chart below.

Overview Identifying Cause and Effect in Fiction

Directions and Sample Answers for Activity Pages

Day 1	See "Provide a Real-World Example" below.
Day 2	Discuss the pictures. Then help students cut out the causes and glue them before the correct effects. (**First:** stepping on sharp rock/wearing a bandage. **Second:** seeing droopy flowers/watering the flowers. **Third:** being hungry/eating an apple.)
Day 3	Read the causes. Discuss. Then help students draw or write an effect for each cause. (Responses will vary.)
Day 4	Read the story together. Discuss the causes and effects. Then help students color in the circle in front of the best answer to each question. (**1:** she was afraid of mice. **2:** she wanted Eve to know she was nice. **3:** she was not afraid anymore.)
Day 5	Read the story together. Ask students to write or draw one of the causes and effects on their graphic organizers. Afterward, meet individually with students to discuss their results. Use their responses to plan further instruction and review. (**First:** Jed spilled milk. He will wipe it up. **Second:** Jed left the TV on. He will turn it off. **Third:** May left pink socks on the stairs. She will pick them up.)

Provide a Real-World Example

◆ Hand out the Day 1 activity page.

◆ Place a book at the edge of your desk. "Accidentally" bump the book and knock it off. **Say:** *I bumped the book. Bumping the book was a cause. A cause is why something happens. Find the picture of someone bumping a book. Put a C in the box for* **cause**.

◆ After students mark the picture, **say:** *The book falling was an effect. An effect is what happens. Find the picture of the book on the floor. Put an E in the box for* **effect**.

◆ Point out the picture of the girl walking on an icy sidewalk. **Say:** *The icy sidewalk is a cause. Put a C in the box. What could happen because of the icy sidewalk?*

◆ Lead students to determine that the girl could slip and fall. Ask them to draw a picture of this effect and then mark the picture with an **E**.

◆ Explain that they can also find causes and effects when they read. Write the following on chart paper:

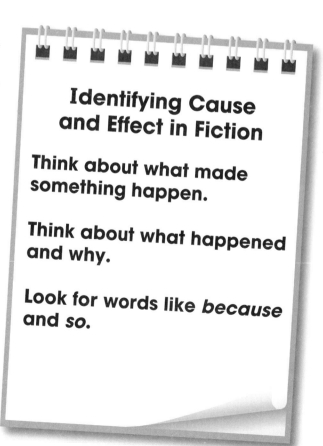

Identifying Cause and Effect in Fiction

Think about what made something happen.

Think about what happened and why.

Look for words like *because* and *so*.

Falling

Mark the picture that shows the cause with a C.

Mark the picture that shows the effect with an E.

Look at the picture. Draw the effect. Then mark each box with a C or an E.

Why?

Cut out each cause below. Glue it before the correct effect.

What Happened?

Read each cause. Draw or write an effect.

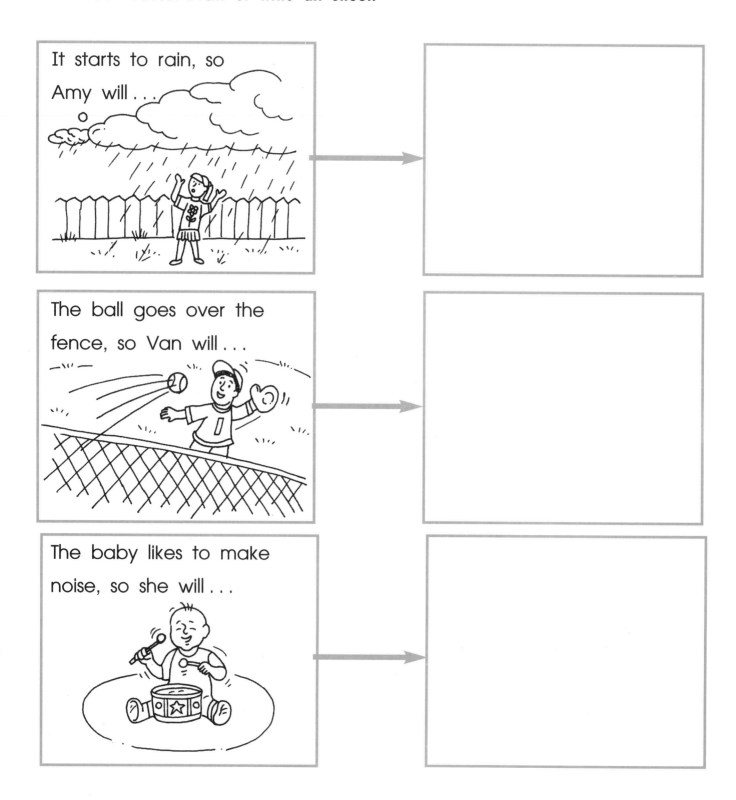

It starts to rain, so Amy will . . .

The ball goes over the fence, so Van will . . .

The baby likes to make noise, so she will . . .

Nice Mice

Read the story.

Mother went into Eve's room.

Eve screamed.

"Why are you screaming?" asked Mother .

"I'm afraid of  ," said Eve.

"I'm a nice  ," said Mother .

"My children are nice , too."

"I won't be afraid, then," said Eve.

"You can even live in my !"

Read the questions. Color in the circle in front of the best answers.

1. Eve screamed because _____.

   ○ she was afraid of mice

   ○ she did not like children

2. Mother mouse talked to Eve because _____.

   ○ she wanted a house

   ○ she wanted Eve to know she was nice

3. Eve let the mice live in her dollhouse because _____.

   ○ she did not like to scream

   ○ she was not afraid anymore

Assessment

Read each passage. Then draw or write the cause and effect.

"Who spilled the ?" asked Dad.
milk

"Jed did, so he will wipe it up," said May.

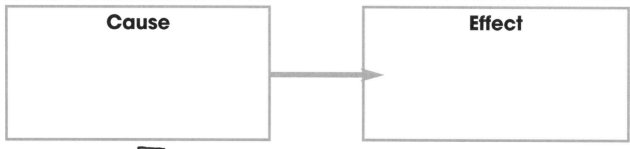

Cause	Effect

"Who left the on?" asked Mom.
TV

"Jed did, so he will turn it off," said May.

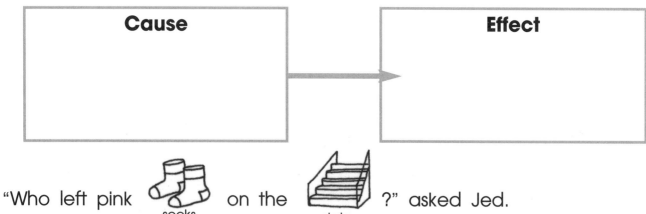

Cause	Effect

"Who left pink socks on the stairs ?" asked Jed.

Dad and Mom looked at May.

"I did, so I'll pick them up," said May.

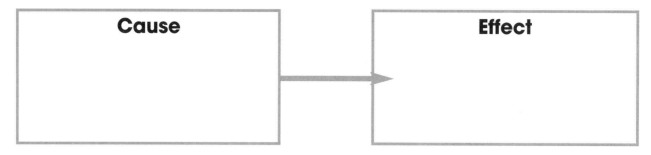

Cause	Effect

Overview Identifying Cause and Effect in Nonfiction

Directions and Sample Answers for Activity Pages

Day 1	See "Provide a Real-World Example" below.
Day 2	Brainstorm things that have happened at school today. Discuss what caused these things to happen. Then help students write or draw one of the cause-and-effect relationships. (Responses will vary.)
Day 3	Read each cause and effect. Discuss. Remind students that a cause happens first, and then the effect happens. Then help students circle the correct causes and effects. (**Cause:** People like to eat corn. **Effect:** Farmers grow it. **Cause:** It got lots of rain. **Effect:** The corn grew tall.)
Day 4	Read the passage together. Discuss the causes and effects. Then help students color in the circle in front of the best answer to each question. (**1:** he needed wood. **2:** she traded her extra wood. **3:** they still need things.)
Day 5	Read the passage together. Ask students to write or draw one of the causes and effects on their graphic organizers. Afterward, meet individually with students to discuss their results. Use their responses to plan further instruction and review. (**First:** we want games to be fair. We have rules. **Second:** We need to know what to do at school. We have rules. **Third:** We need to be safe on the street. We have rules.)

Provide a Real-World Example

◆ Hand out the Day 1 activity page.

◆ Ask students to cut out the big square. Together, fold the squares in half. Then fold them in half once again to form small squares. **Say:** *Making something happen is a cause. Folding the big square twice is a cause. The thing that happens is an effect. Making a small square is an effect.* Write the word **small** on the board and ask students to write it on the line. Then read the cause and effect together.

◆ Ask students to unfold their papers. **Say:** *Something happened when we unfolded our papers. What happened?* Allow time for students to discuss that unfolding the paper revealed four small squares. Point out that unfolding the paper was a cause, and seeing four small squares was the effect. Ask students to write the numeral **4** on the line, and then read the cause and effect together.

◆ Explain that they can also find causes and effects when they read. Write the following on chart paper:

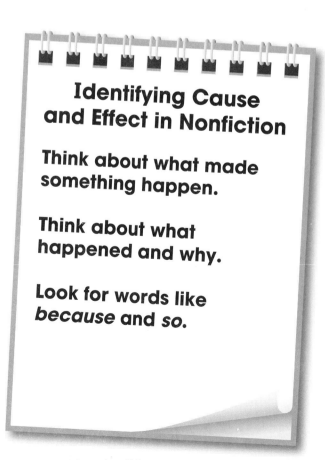

Identifying Cause and Effect in Nonfiction

Think about what made something happen.

Think about what happened and why.

Look for words like *because* and *so.*

Squares

Cut out the square below. Then fold it in half twice.

Cause: I folded the big square twice.

Effect: I made a _____ square.

Cause: I unfolded the paper.

Effect: I saw _____ squares.

Today at School

Think of something that happened at school today. Think about what caused it to happen. Write or draw the cause and effect below.

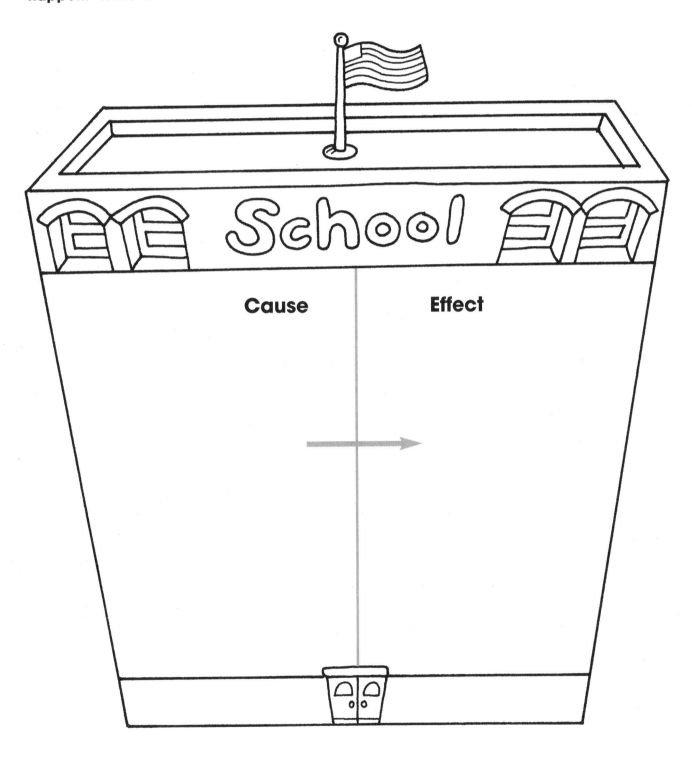

Cause   Effect

Growing Corn

Read each cause and effect. Then read the questions.
Draw a circle around the best answers.

1. People like to eat corn, **so** farmers grow it.

   What is the cause?

   People like to eat .
   corn

   Farmers grow it.

   What is the effect?

   People like to eat .
   corn

   Farmers grow it.

2. The corn grew tall, **because** it got lots of rain.

   What is the cause?

   The  grew tall.
   corn

   It got lots of rain.

   What is the effect?

   The grew tall.
   corn

   It got lots of rain.

Trading

Read the passage.

Long ago, people traded for things they needed.

A man needed wood . He had extra .
fish

A woman needed . She had extra .
fish   wood

The man and the woman traded.

People still trade for things they need today.

You might have an extra .
pencil

Your friend might have an extra .
eraser

You can trade!

Read the questions. Color in the circle in front of the best answers.

1. The man traded his extra fish, because _____.

   ○ he needed
   wood
   ○ he needed more
   fish

2. The woman needed fish so _____.

   ○ she got extra
   fish
   ○ she traded her extra
   wood

3. People still trade things today, because _____.

   ○ they still need things

   ○ they have extra and
   fish   wood

Assessment

We have rules when we play games.

These rules keep the games fair.

We have rules at school.

These rules help us know what to do.

We have rules on the street.

These rules keep us safe.

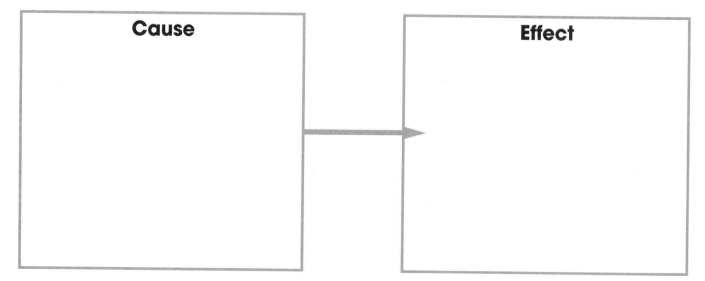

Cause	**Effect**

Overview Making Inferences in Fiction

Directions and Sample Answers for Activity Pages

Day 1	See "Provide a Real-World Example" below.
Day 2	Discuss the picture. Then help students draw or write their ideas on the chart and circle the best inference. (**Picture clue:** Cam is getting an umbrella. **What I already know:** We use umbrellas in the rain. **Inference:** It is raining outside.)
Day 3	Read the sentences together. Discuss. Then help students draw or write their ideas in the boxes. (**Sentence clues:** A man is feeding an elephant. **What I already know:** Zoos have elephants. **Inference:** The boy and his dad are at the zoo.)
Day 4	Read the story together. Discuss. Then help students circle the best answer to each question. (**Story clues:** The girl went to the swings. The girl got ice cream. **What I already know:** Ice cream can melt. **Inference:** The girl ate the ice cream and then got on the swings.)
Day 5	Read the story together. Ask students to write or draw clues about what Jen is doing and what they already know about the clues. Then ask them to make an inference about what Jen is pointing at. Afterward, meet individually with students to discuss their results. Use their responses to plan further instruction and review. (**Clues:** Jen's birthday is January 20. Jen points at the wall. **What I already know:** January 20 is on a calendar. Calendars are on walls. **Inference:** Jen is pointing at a calendar.)

Provide a Real-World Example

◆ Hand out the Day 1 activity page.

◆ **Say:** *I will pretend I am getting ready for school. First, I will choose a shirt. I have a red shirt and a blue shirt. Color my two shirts.*

◆ Allow time for students to color the two shirts.

◆ **Say:** *I will choose the blue shirt. Draw a circle around the blue shirt. Next, I will choose a pair of socks. I have blue socks and green socks. Color my two pairs of socks.*

◆ Allow time for students to color the two pairs of socks.

◆ **Say:** *I will choose the blue socks. Draw a circle around the blue socks.*

◆ **Say:** *The blue shirt and blue socks are clues. You know something about choosing colors, too. Think about the clues and what you already know. Can you make a good guess, or inference, about what color I like?*

◆ Allow time for students to discuss their ideas and then complete the sentence at the bottom of the page. They should infer that you like the color blue. Then explain that they can also make inferences when they read. Write the following on chart paper:

Making Inferences in Fiction

Find clues in the pictures.

Find clues in the words.

Think about what you already know.

What Color Do I Like?

Listen to the instructions. Color the shirts. Next color the socks. Then circle the shirt and socks that are chosen.

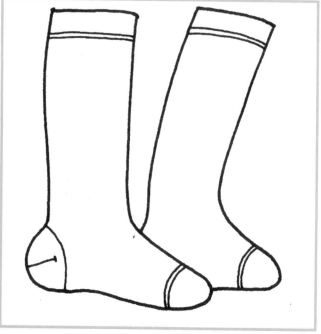

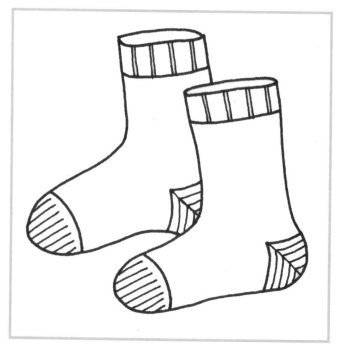

Inference:

I like _____.

Cam's Umbrella

Look at the picture. Then draw or write your ideas on the chart.

Clues in the Picture	What I Already Know

Draw a circle around the best inference.

Cam wants to play outside.

It is raining outside.

Out with Dad

Read the sentences. Then draw or write your ideas in the boxes.

Dad and I saw a man.

He was feeding an .

elephant

I know from the sentences that . . .	**I already know . . .**

I can make an inference. The boy and his dad are at the . . .

At the Park

Read the story.

We went to the  .
park

I went to the .
swings

We got .
ice cream

Which clues are in the story? Draw a circle around your answers.

The girl saw .
swings

The girl got on the .
swings

The girl got .
ice cream

What do you already know? Draw a circle around your answer.

All kids get on the 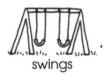 .
swings

 can melt.
Ice cream

What did the girl do? Draw a circle around the best inference.

The girl ate the and then got on the .
ice cream   swings

The girl got on the and then ate the .
swings   ice cream

Assessment

Read the passage.

It was cold outside. Jen's class had recess inside.

"I don't like winter," said Sam. "I want to play outside."

"I like winter," said Jen. "My birthday is in winter. My birthday is January 20."

Jen pointed at the wall. "Look! My birthday is tomorrow!"

Write your ideas in the boxes below.

Clues	What I Already Know

Inference

Overview Making Inferences in Nonfiction

Directions and Sample Answers for Activity Pages

Day 1	See "Provide a Real-World Example" below.
Day 2	Discuss the picture. Then help students draw or write their ideas on the chart and circle the best inference. (**Evidence in picture:** A teacher wrote 1 + 7 on the board. **What I already know:** 1 + 7 = 8. **Inference:** The teacher will write 8 under the line.)
Day 3	Read the sentences together. Discuss. Then help students draw or write their ideas in the boxes. (**Evidence in sentence:** A mountain can have snow on top. **What I already know:** Cold places have snow. **Inference:** The top of a mountain is cold.)
Day 4	Read the weather report together. Discuss. Then help students circle the best answer to each question. (**Evidence in weather report:** Lightning is all over town. The town will not have a baseball game. **What I already know:** Lightning is not safe. **Inference:** People would not be safe at the baseball game.)
Day 5	Read the letter together. Ask students to write or draw evidence from Osa's letter and what they already know about the evidence. Then ask them to make an inference about what type of pet Osa wants. Afterward, meet individually with students to discuss their results. Use their responses to plan further instruction and review. (**Evidence:** Osa wants a pet. Osa would take the pet for walks. **What I already know:** Dogs are pets. Dogs need to go for walks. **Inference:** Osa wants a dog.)

Provide a Real-World Example

◆ Hand out the Day 1 activity page.

◆ **Say:** *I will pretend I have two pretzels. Draw two pretzels on the tray.*

◆ Allow time for students to draw two pretzels.

◆ **Say:** *Now I will pretend that my neighbor comes over. The two pretzels and my neighbor are evidence. You know something about pretzels and neighbors, too. Think about the evidence and what you already know. Can you make a good guess, or inference, about what I will do next? Draw your idea in the box.*

◆ Allow time for students to draw and discuss their ideas. They should infer that you will give one of the pretzels to your neighbor. Then explain that they can also make inferences when they read. Write the following on chart paper:

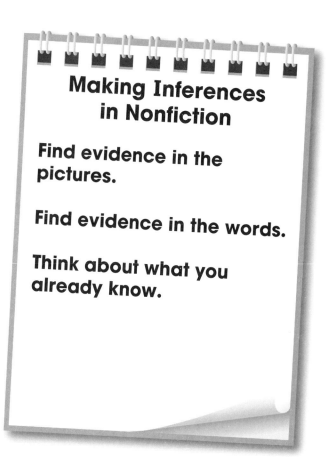

Making Inferences in Nonfiction

Find evidence in the pictures.

Find evidence in the words.

Think about what you already know.

Two Pretzels

Draw two pretzels. Then draw or write your inference in the box.

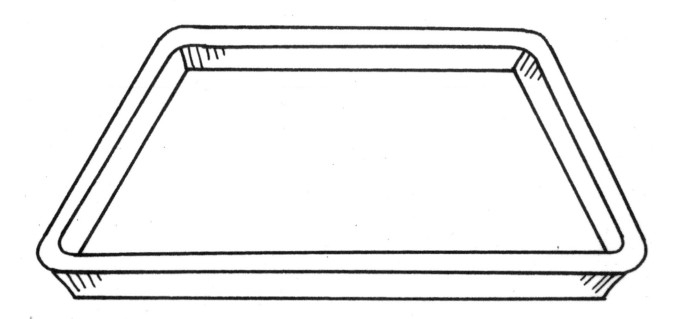

┌ ─ ┐

Inference

└ ─ ┘

Adding Up

Look at the picture. Then draw or write your ideas on the chart.

Evidence in the Picture	**What I Already Know**

Draw a circle around the best inference.

Teachers like to add.

The teacher will write 8 under the line.

Mountain Tops

Read the sentences.
Then draw or write your ideas in the boxes.

Have you ever seen a mountain?

Many mountains have snow at the top.

I know from the sentences that _____.

I already know _____.

I can make an inference. The top of a mountain is _____.

Weather Report

Read the weather report.

Which evidence is in the weather report? Draw a circle around your answers.

What do you already know? Draw a circle around your answer.

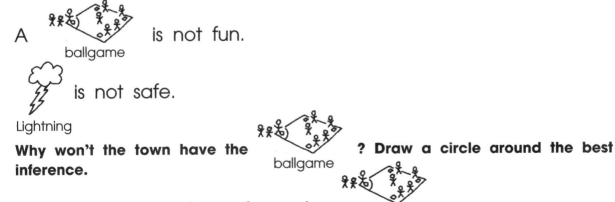

A ballgame is not fun.

Lightning is not safe.

Why won't the town have the ballgame **? Draw a circle around the best inference.**

People would not be safe at the ballgame .

People would not have fun at the ballgame .

Assessment

Read the note.

Dear Mom,

I think I should have a pet. I would play with my pet.

I would give my pet food and water.

I would take my pet for walks.

Please let me have a pet.

Love,

Osa

Write your ideas below.

Evidence	**What I Already Know**

Inference

Overview Drawing Conclusions in Fiction

Directions and Sample Answers for Activity Pages

Day 1	See "Provide a Real-World Example" below.
Day 2	Read each character description. Help students use the clues to draw a conclusion about who or what the character might be. Then help students cut out the pictures and glue each character in the right box. (**First:** baby. **Second:** clown. **Third:** monkey.)
Day 3	Read the story together. Discuss. Help students circle the best conclusion. Then help them circle the clues they used from the story. (**Conclusion:** Gus and Tia are friends. **Clues:** Gus is having a family picnic. Tia's brother is coming for a visit. Gus and Tia go to the same school.)
Day 4	Read the story together. Discuss. Help students draw or write Leo's conclusion. Then help them circle the clues that Leo used. (**Conclusion:** A bird left the feather on the bed. **Clues:** The window was open. A tree was outside the window. A nest was in the tree. The nest had a feather in it.)
Day 5	Read the story together. Ask students to write or draw clues about the map. Then ask them to write or draw a conclusion. Afterward, meet individually with students to discuss their results. Use their responses to plan further instruction and review. (**Clues:** The kitchen looks like Dot's kitchen. The bedrooms look like Dot's bedrooms. The bathroom and hallway look like Dot's bathroom and hallway. **Conclusion:** Dot found a map of her own house.)

Provide a Real-World Example

◆ Hand out the Day 1 activity page.

◆ **Say:** *My friend could not find her watch. She thought about the day before. She put on her watch in the morning. She wore it all day at work. Then she went home and made dinner. After dinner, she washed the dishes. She never wears her watch when she washes the dishes. She always puts her watch on the windowsill. Once she thought of all these clues, she knew where to find her watch. She found her watch on the windowsill.*

◆ Help students circle the clues that the friend thought of. Then give them time to draw the watch on the windowsill.

◆ **Say:** *Using several clues to figure something out is called drawing a conclusion.* Then explain that students can also draw conclusions when they read stories. Write the following on chart paper:

Drawing Conclusions in Fiction

Find clues in the pictures.

Find clues in the words.

Think about what makes sense based on the clues.

The Missing Watch

Listen to the story. Circle the clues in the story. Then draw where she found the watch below.

Characters Who Make Us Smile

Read about each character. Use the clues to draw a conclusion about the character.

People smile when they see me!

I like to eat, sleep, and play.

I can't walk yet.

People smile when they see me!

I wear funny clothes.

I like to have fun.

People smile when they see me!

I do funny tricks.

I like to climb trees.

Cut out the pictures. Glue each character in the right box.

Gus and Tia

Read the story.

Gus saw Tia. "We're having a ," said Gus.

"That sounds like fun!" said Tia.

"Would you like to come with me?" asked Gus.

"I can't. My brother is coming for a visit," said Tia.

"OK," said Gus. "I'll see you at Monday!"

Which is the best conclusion? Draw a circle around your answer.

Gus is Tia's brother.

Gus and Tia are friends.

Which clues are in the story? Draw a circle around your answers.

Gus is having a .

Tia is having a .

Gus's brother is coming for a visit.

Tia's brother is coming for a visit.

Gus and Tia go to the same .

Gus and Tia go to the same .

The Mystery of the Feather

Read the story.

Leo woke up.

A  was on his bed!
feather

"How could a  get on my bed?"
feather

he asked.

Leo looked around.

The 🪟 was open.
window

A 🌳 was outside the 🪟 .
tree   window

A 🪺 was in the 🌳 .
nest   tree

The 🪺 had a 🪶 in it.
nest   feather

"Now I know!" said Leo.

What did Leo conclude? Draw or write your answer.

[blank box]

What clues did Leo use? Draw a circle around the clues in the story.

Assessment

Read the story.

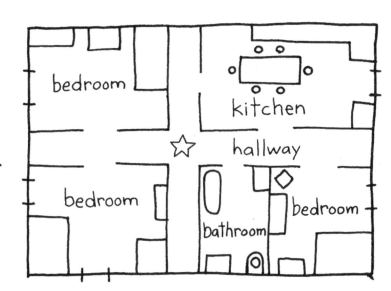

"I found a map!" said Dot.

"What is on the map?" asked Dad.

"I see a kitchen. It looks like our kitchen!" said Dot.

"I see three bedrooms, too. They look like our bedrooms!"

"Do you see a bathroom and hallway?" asked Dad.

"Do they look like our bathroom and hallway?"

"Yes!" said Dot.

Use clues from the story to draw a conclusion.

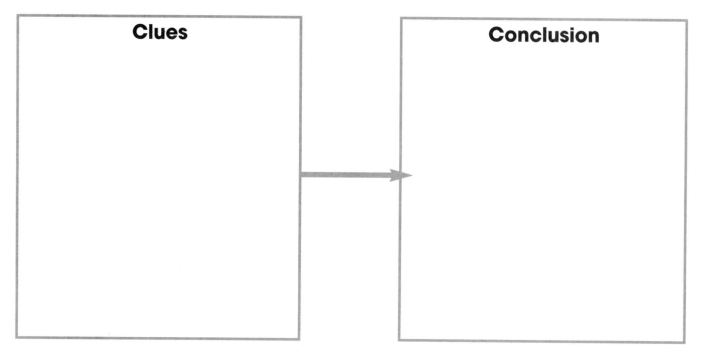

Overview Drawing Conclusions in Nonfiction

Directions and Sample Answers for Activity Pages

Day 1	See "Provide a Real-World Example" below.
Day 2	Read the description of each place. Help students use the clues to draw a conclusion about what the place might be. Then help students cut out the pictures and glue each place in the right box. (**First:** city. **Second:** farm. **Third:** lake.)
Day 3	Read the passage together. Discuss. Help students select the best conclusion. Then help them circle the evidence they used from the passage. (**Conclusion:** Extreme weather is not safe. **Evidence:** To be safe . . . stay inside if a blizzard is coming; go to a shelter if a tornado is coming; leave if a hurricane is coming.)
Day 4	Read the passage together. Discuss. Help students draw or write their conclusion. Then help them circle the evidence they used from the passage. (**Conclusion:** My pencil is a solid. **Evidence:** A solid has a shape. A solid has a size. You can see a solid. You can touch a solid.)
Day 5	Read the passage together. Ask students to write or draw evidence from the passage in the first box and their conclusion in the second box. Afterward, meet individually with students to discuss their results. Use their responses to plan further instruction and review. (**Evidence:** Sometimes it's better to multiply. 10 pages + 10 pages + 10 pages + 10 pages + 10 pages = 50 pages. 5 books x 10 pages = 50 pages. **Conclusion:** Multiplying is faster.)

Provide a Real-World Example

◆ Hand out the Day 1 activity page.

◆ **Say:** *We had a visitor to the school cafeteria. He noticed many things. He saw kids sitting together. He saw kids smiling and laughing. He saw kids helping each other. He heard kids saying "Please" and "Thank You." He heard kids making plans to play together after school. My friend thought about all this evidence. He figured out that the kids in our school are friendly.*

◆ Ask students to draw another place at your school where a visitor might see friendly kids. Then help them fill in the word **friendly** to complete the conclusion and read it together.

◆ **Say:** *Using several pieces of evidence to figure something out is called drawing a conclusion.* Then explain that students can also draw conclusions when they read. Write the following on chart paper:

Drawing Conclusions in Nonfiction

Find evidence in the pictures.

Find evidence in the words.

Think about what makes sense based on the evidence.

Our Friendly School

Listen to the story about our friendly school.

Draw another place where students at your school are friendly.

[blank drawing box]

Conclusion:

The kids in our school are _____.

Places People Like to Live

**Read about each place. Use the evidence
to draw a conclusion about the place.**

People like to live here!

Some people live in apartments.

Some people ride a bus to work.

People like to live here!

Some people grow corn.

Some people have cows.

People like to live here!

Some people have boats.

Some people catch fish.

Cut out the pictures. Glue each picture in the right box.

Extreme Weather

Read the passage.

Sometimes weather can be extreme.

A [blizzard] is extreme weather. People stay inside to be safe.

A [tornado] is extreme weather. People go to a shelter to be safe.

A [hurricane] is extreme weather. People leave to be safe.

Which is the best conclusion? Draw a circle around your answer.

A [blizzard] is safe.

A [tornado] is safer than a [hurricane] .

Extreme weather is not safe.

Which evidence is in the passage? Draw a circle around your answers.

To be safe . . .

stay inside if a  is coming.

stay inside if a is coming.

go to a shelter if a is coming.

go to a shelter if a is coming.

leave if a is coming.

leave if a is coming.

   Unit 20 • Everyday Comprehension Intervention Activities Grade 1 • ©2010 Newmark Learning, LLC

Solids

Read the passage.

A solid has a shape.

A solid has a size.

You can see a solid.

You can touch a solid.

Your desk is a solid.

Your paper is a solid.

Is your pencil a solid?

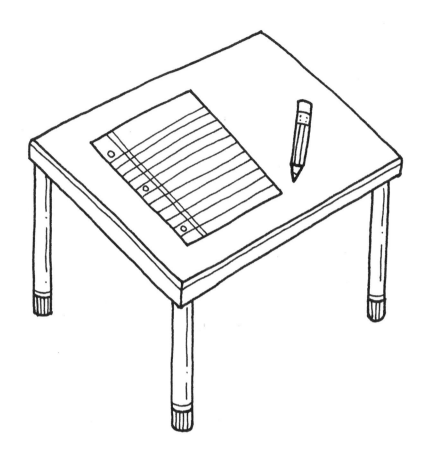

What can you conclude about your pencil? Write your answer.

_____

_____

_____

What evidence did you use? Draw a circle around the evidence in the passage.

Assessment

**Read the passages. Then draw
a conclusion.**

Sometimes we add.

Sometimes it's better to multiply.

Here are 5 books.

Each book has 10 pages.

Let's add.

10 pages + 10 pages + 10 pages + 10 pages + 10 pages = 50 pages.

Now, let's multiply.

5 books x 10 pages = 50 pages.

Which is faster?

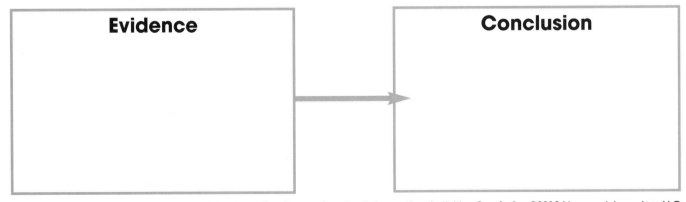

Evidence	Conclusion

Notes

Notes